For more information on the life and legacy of Patrick Wesley Wheeler or to share stories of how this book has impacted your life please email us at pwheelslegacy@gmail.com

or

Visit: servingwith7.blogspot.com

or

Follow us on Instagram @Servingiwth7

#KeepItMoving

GOOD MORNING,
MEN OF GOD

Patrick Wesley Wheeler

This book is dedicated

To the husbands and fathers trying to love God, and your families:

be encouraged and lean into Him for your strength.

To our children:

be who God has called you to be, no matter what.

To each and every one reading this book:

you were preserved for a purpose.

#KeepItMoving

INTRODUCTION

In my eyes, Patrick was a superhuman, God's favorite, and a natural encourager. One of his most unique and astonishing qualities was his genuine gifting to inspire others. It was truly who he was. Patrick was everyone's hype man. If you had any doubt that you could do great things, he would root you on and see you through.

Over the span of nearly twenty years, Patrick was my very best friend, true love, partner, pastor, and proud father to my children. As my husband and true compliment, I often told him "it was either you, or no one". He was patient when I was pressed; energized when I was exhausted; hopeful when I was hesitant. He always made sure that the kids and I felt loved and prioritized.

All kids loved Patrick. He was a big teddy bear and a fun-loving guy. Often touted as the "baby whisperer," he was known to lull many a baby to sleep with his soothing, baritone voice. He was loved especially by his children, who would greet him with a resounding, "Daddy!" every time he walked through the door. Watching him with our children was a faith phenomenon. He was always full of energy, ideas, and fun. I watched him deal delicately, listen intently, and pour into each one of them so passionately. Growing up without a father myself, I was astounded at how much joy he brought to their lives by simply walking through the door. He was theirs, and it was a beautiful model of the Heavenly Father's love for us.

The morning Patrick went into the hospital, he was spending time with his children and modeling servant leadership for them by shopping for fresh produce to share with the neighbors in the mobile home park. The children always looked forward to going out with him to share the love of Jesus in the community.

He emulated the love and light of Jesus in a very practical way. He often quoted John 3:17: "For God did not send his Son into the world to condemn the world, but to save the world through him". He wanted people to know that God's love for them was all-consuming. We worked side by side in earning our master's degrees in biblical counseling to be better equipped to minister in the margins. Spending more than half of his life doing outreach ministry, reaching people where they were was important to him. His calling seemed to be creating a safe space where people felt seen. Our sister in the faith, Deborah, said it best: "Patrick was the feet, hands, and voice of God that poured love on the unloved".

Patrick never met a stranger, and after ten minutes with him, you felt like you'd gained a new best friend. He was so very genuine, kind, humble and funny. Many experienced him as a devoted friend, brother, and pastor.

During his tenure as a Sales Manager and later a Corporate Trainer in the field of logistics, his gift of encouragement shone even brighter. He was often dubbed the "camp counselor" as he would motivate, uplift, and inspire. He truly cared about his colleagues and their success, not only on the job, but in life. A former colleague, Adam shared: "Patrick was an incredible man that challenged me to grow in faith and in family". One of his last accomplishments on the job as Director of Logistics was helping to implement a Mental Health Initiative. He helped to carry a part of everyone's pain and story as his own.

Whether he was at a little league game, helping strangers push their cars to safety on the side of the road, having lunch with a coworker, or walking through at-risk neighborhoods, he was always sharing the love and light of Jesus. When Patrick was promoted to Heaven, one of our friends put it best: "the world will be a little darker without him here".

This book was written with you in mind. I'm a witness. In every test, trial, and triumph of his life, Patrick longed to share with others. He would often say: "When I get on the other side of this, I'm going to write a book. I want to help somebody."

In these pages, I hope that you will not only find inspiration, but that you feel the very warmth of a friend in the faith walking alongside you on the road of being refined by the Blessed Redeemer. He is for you.

Keisha L. Wheeler

YOU ARE THE *ONE*

I therefore, a prisoner for the Lord, urge you to walk in a manner worthy of the calling to which you have been called.

Ephesians 4:1 ESV

Good Morning, Men of God!

Nobody is more equipped to lead your family than you. Regardless of how hard it is sometimes, God has uniquely equipped and positioned you as the head of your household. It was not by accident. Nobody can take the authority God has given you. There are no rivals. You submit to God the Father for guidance. Your family follows your lead. Being a father and/or husband is a calling. It is a gift from God.

You must make sure that your life reflects your understanding of the importance of this calling. You will never have all the answers. You will never get everything right. Your determination to lead effectively must be demonstrated in your dedication to proper preparation. If you say you want to lose weight, but never exercise and you eat like a pig, you're not dedicated to losing weight. In the same manner, you can't say you want to be the husband and father your family needs without doing the work. As a Godly man, your prayer, reading, worship, and serving time must be a foundation of your life. You can't be content with morning devotionals. Your resolve to be equipped as a leader demands that you seek the Father with reckless abandon. Make it a priority today. There is no other way to accept the call to headship, but on your knees in prayer.

Let us pray: *Thank You Lord, for establishing me as the head of my family under You. Please guide me in every aspect of leadership as I seek You to know how to be the father and husband You have called me to be. Thank You for my family. Please allow my dedication to a life committed to You to be an example to them. I praise You, Jesus. Thank You! In Jesus Christ's name I pray, Amen.*

Love you guys,

Patrick

YOU ARE THE JOY

Looking to Jesus, the founder and perfector of our faith, who for the joy that was set before him endured the cross, despising the shame, and is seated at the right hand of the throne of God.

Hebrews 12:2 ESV

Good Morning, Men of God!

During Christmas and Easter, I always think about the hours before the death of Jesus Christ. The fact that my Savior was abandoned by His closest friends, endured excruciating pain, and was separated from God the Father is astounding to me. From the moment He entered the world He was destined to die to pay for the sins of the entirety of humanity.

The text today tells us that Jesus endured the cross for the *joy* that was set before Him. As you go into today, understand that you are the joy that was set before the Lord that enabled Him to endure the cross. The thought of an eternity with you was the driving force behind His sacrifice. Being reconnected with you made it worth the nails in His hands and feet.

Saving you from yourself was worth the excessive beating and ridicule. He investigated the future, saw you, and it gave him Enduring Joy!

That is worth a celebration all by itself. My hope for you today is that you acknowledge your worth in God's eyes. The value of an object is based on how much someone is willing to pay for it. Jesus paid the ultimate price for you. Regardless of what you are going through today, no matter the obstacle you are trying to climb over today, walk in the joy of the Lord, knowing that God's plan for you is perfect. He did not endure the cross to allow you to be defeated or devoured by the enemy. Take comfort in His Enduring Joy.

Let us pray: *Thank You, Jesus, for valuing me so highly. I am not worthy, but I am very grateful. I surrender to You the plan for my life purpose. Thank You for being my peace and sustaining joy. Please guide me in seeing and serving you in all aspects of life. In Jesus Christ's name I pray, Amen.*

Love you guys,

Patrick

UNDERSTANDING THAT YOU WON'T ALWAYS UNDERSTAND

For my thoughts are not your thoughts, neither are your ways my ways, declares the Lord. For as the heavens are higher than the earth, so are my ways higher than your ways and my thoughts than your thoughts.

Isaiah 55:8-9 ESV

Good Morning, Men of God!

We have all dealt with our fair share of tragedy. There have been hardships in life that have affected those most important to us. Circumstances have brought us to a place where we wonder if God is watching. Does He care? How could He let this happen?

God's thoughts and ways are not our thoughts and ways. He sees the eternity of His entire creation in one cohesive narrative. We will never understand everything. If we could, why would we need God?

13

What we do know is the truth about God. He loves you. He sacrificed Himself in the form of His Son Jesus to save you. He does not delight in your pain, nor is He excited at your hardship. Trust Him. Trust His process. It really comes down to that. Do you truly believe God loves you and has your best interest at heart? Do you truly believe that He is Sovereign? Hopefully your honest answer to those questions is "yes", but if it is "no", understand that God loves you and knows exactly where you are. He understands your struggle and offers you His unrelenting peace, care, and compassion.

Let us pray: *Dear God, I do not have to understand the way my life moves and adjusts. Please guide me in trusting you no matter the changes and adjustments. Only You are worthy, God, of my praise. Lead me, Father! In Jesus Christ's name I pray, Amen!*

Love you guys,

Patrick

PERFECT PEACE

You keep him in perfect peace whose mind is stayed on you,
because he trusts in you.

Isaiah 26:3 ESV

Good Morning, Men of God!

What is imperfect peace? It is when we partially believe in God's power. We believe enough to trust Him to wake us up, but not enough to trust that He will be our refuge. We believe He created the sun and the moon, but our anxieties are out of His reach. We believe in Him to sustain our breath, but not enough to trust His provision. To stand as a husband and father, there are some spiritual non-negotiables. The most important is truly keeping our minds on God and trusting in Him. The stresses, distractions, and temptations are many. The attack from Satan is unending. Confusion, depression, and defeat crouch at the door, waiting for us every day.

Our text tells us that He will keep us in Perfect Peace, whose mind stays on Him. Centering our focus on God is the perfect display of our trust in Him. It not only ignites our purpose, but it also brings us to a place of balanced peace. Stress and anxiety destroy our bodies and mind. Allowing ourselves to be engulfed in these things prevents us from experiencing life with the joy God intended. God designed us to trust in Him. Allow Him to solidify you in perfect peace today. Keep your mind stayed on Him.

Let us pray: *Father there are so many distractions. So much to be concerned about. Please help me today to focus on You. You see me. You see the circumstances that stand in my path. I place my trust completely in You. Please allow me to rest in Your perfect peace, regardless of my circumstance. Thank You, Lord! In Jesus Christ's name I pray, Amen.*

Love you guys,

Patrick

SECURE FOUNDATION

For you have forgotten the God of your salvation and have not remembered the Rock of your refuge; therefore, though you plant pleasant plants and sow the vine-branch of a stranger, though you make them grow on the day that you plant them and make them blossom in the morning that you sow, yet the harvest will flee away in a day of grief and incurable pain.

Isaiah 17:10-11 ESV

Good Morning, Men of God!

Enduring hardship is a part of life. Regardless of what stage of life we are at or the responsibilities we have, it is a guarantee that a part of our journey will be dealing with pain that causes sadness but also encourages physical, emotional, and spiritual growth.

Our text this morning is another reminder of where our focus should be. We know that Satan is attacking and hardships loom. We must reflect on this truth. God is our Protector. He is our Defender. He is our Salvation, Hope and Foundation. It is our security in Him that gives us the hope and faith that enables us to endure hardship. If we build our lives and chase success without acknowledging God as Sovereign ruler and Lord over our lives, then what we acquire is almost certainly forecasted to be dashed away. When we allow God to guide us, we are secure even in the day of grief and incurable pain. Anchor yourself and hope in the God who is your refuge today!

Let us pray: *Father, You endured hardship as an example to Your children. As I follow Your footsteps, please allow me to find refuge in You this day. Direct me on this road as I encounter hardship, that even in times of pain, You get the Glory, Lord. Hallelujah Jesus. In Jesus Christ's name I pray, Amen.*

Love you guys,

Patrick

CHRIST-LIKE LEADERSHIP

Therefore, since we are surrounded by so great a cloud of witnesses, let us also lay aside every weight, and sin which clings so closely, and let us run with endurance the race that is set before us.

Hebrews 12:1 ESV

Good Morning, Men of God!

Who is your great cloud of witnesses? Who are the people God has called your life to influence? I meditate on this scripture a lot. I start with my kids, then it expands to other people I pray for daily outside of my home.

Do you know who I forget? My wife. Sometimes I get in such a flow of doing life with Keisha that I forget that I am supposed to be setting an example for her first. She and I get so focused while managing our large family, that my spiritual focus jumps over her and starts with my kids. Lord, please forgive me! Our wives partner with us to raise our kids and manage our household. We should make their spiritual certainty, personal growth, and affectionate needs our priority. As we are running the race laid out for us, we need to make sure they are seeking God and running their race, right next to us. Our children will have a more stable path to follow if it is laid by two sets of feet. As we climb the mountain towards our Godly purpose, our wives need our care and attention to make sure they are secure on their path as well. A part of loving our wives like Christ loved the Church is leading them the way Christ led the church, by example.

Let us pray: *Jesus thank You so much for my wife. Thank You for her grace and diligence. Please open up my eyes and heart to ways I can admonish and encourage her. Show me her hurt and areas of pain, that I might be used of You to love her through them. Help me to be mindful of how effectively I support and care for her. Thank You, Lord! In Jesus Christ's name I pray, Amen.*

Love you guys,

Patrick

THEY ARE YOUR CREATION

So I went down to the potter's house, and there he was working at his wheel. And the vessel he was making of clay was spoiled in the potter's hand, and he reworked it into another vessel, as it seemed good to the potter to do.

Jeremiah 18:3-4 ESV

Good Morning, Men of God!

We want great things for our families. As fathers and husbands, we want to do our best to guide those in our care into success and happiness. We are willing to sacrifice anything if it means shaping their futures in a positive manner. All of this is honorable, but we must remember that God is the Potter, not us. Our wives and children are on HIS wheel, and HE will shape them as HE sees fit.

Isaiah 64:8 tells us that God is Father and Potter, we are all clay in his hands. Our influence should be used to love and instruct those we love in the ways of the Lord. The best way to "shape" those we love is to direct them to the Cross of Christ. It is in this relationship with the Father that those around us are shaped into who God wants them to be.

Let us pray: *My Loving Father in Heaven, help me to drive my family towards what You have called them to. They belong to You. They are Your creation. Forgive me, please, for leaning toward what I think they should do or accomplish. You know best, Lord. I will lovingly direct them toward You. In Jesus Christ's name I pray, Amen.*

Love you guys,

Patrick

TIME TO ENCOURAGE

Two are better than one, because they have a good reward for their toil. For if they fall, one will lift up his fellow. But woe to his who is alone when he falls and has not another to lift him up!

Ecclesiastes 4:9-10 ESV

Good Morning, Men of God!

We carry a lot of responsibility as husbands and fathers. Men make friends a lot slower than women. We are slow to open and share our concerns, fears, or insecurities. That is why it is very important that we encourage each other. We know what our brothers are going through without them even saying it, because we are going through it too. The bond of Godly Brotherhood is very important.

The text from Ecclesiastes shows us that having someone to walk with us in encouragement and support is helpful. Being alone and blocked off makes us easy prey for Satan. Having a Godly brotherhood helps us to stand even on days when we can't feel our legs. I encourage you today to go out of your way to call, email, or text a word of encouragement to a brother in your spiritual circle. Ask him how you can pray for him and his family this week. Offer yourself as that encouraging support that God can use to ease your brother's roughest days.

Let us pray: *My Lord, please bless me with men of accountability, that I may find prayer and support in hard times. Being a man of God during this time is very difficult. Please help me to find aid and support in my Godly brothers. There is nothing weak about vulnerability. Help me to embrace and even be a crutch of support when needed for my brothers in Christ. Thank You, Lord. In Jesus Christ's name I pray, Amen.*

Love you guys,

Patrick

THE POWER OF PRAYER

And this is the confidence that we have toward him, that if we ask anything according to his will he hears us. And if we know that he hears us in whatever we ask, we know that we have the requests that we have asked of him.

1 John 5:14-15 ESV

Good Morning, Men of God!

If God answers every prayer we prayed today, how many people outside of ourselves would it effect? I heard that question recently, and it really made me think. Prayer is one of the most powerful weapons in our spiritual arsenal. As we spend time seeking God in prayer, we are aligned with His will for our lives. God has given us an avenue of communication through Jesus Christ that allows us to humbly approach the throne to offer confession, thanksgivings, receive forgiveness, and make requests.

As fathers and husbands, let's be sure to pray specifically for our loved ones. Use the gift of prayer to carry not just our circumstances to the Father but ask God to burden our heart with the needs of those around us. Our prayer life dictates what and who we really care about. I challenge you guys today to take time and pray for the specific needs of everyone in your immediate family. Take time and pray for your church, pastor, and leaders. As the Holy Spirit leads your willing heart, use this beautiful gift of prayer to affect the lives of those around you.

Let us pray: *God, my Father in Heaven, thank You for the ability to approach Your throne with prayer. I realize that it is the blood of Jesus and His resurrection that gives me this opportunity. Lord, as I pray this week, and today, please burden my heart with the needs of those around me. Help me to remember to pray for others as fervently as I pray for myself. Thank You, Lord. In Jesus Christ's name I pray, Amen.*

Love you guys,

Patrick

QUALIFIED EXAMPLE

Do your best to present yourself to God as one approved, a worker who has no need to be ashamed, rightly handling the word of truth.

2 Timothy 2:15 ESV

Good Morning, Men of God!

Have you ever had a boss or supervisor that was unqualified to lead you? How did you feel when they gave you instructions? Whether you followed their lead or not, you probably felt a little uneasy about their ability to lead you.

In our text today, Paul is instructing Timothy to study to show himself approved. In other words, Paul is telling him to study to show his qualifications to give instructions/lead the people Paul was sending Timothy to teach on his behalf. The clear fact is that people have an easier time following leaders when they have confidence in their qualifications. This thought should drive us into our Bible every day. It should propel us into morning worship. It demands that we study to show ourselves approved as fathers and husbands. Our families will follow our lead to seek the Lord a lot better when they see us seeking. Our wives will trust our leadership when they know we are fervently pursuing God for guidance. Set the example for your family the way Paul urged Timothy to lead those in his care.

Let us pray: *Dear Jesus, Thank You for setting the perfect example of life and love. Thank You for the work, diligence, and intentional nature You committed towards making sure that I have a Godly example to follow. Please guide me in replicating Your example and living a life that inspires my family to seek and serve You. In Jesus Christ's name I pray, Amen!*

Love you guys,

Patrick

CORRECT RESPONSE

While walking by the Sea of Galilee, he saw two brothers, Simon (who is called Peter) and Andrew his brother, casting a net into the sea, for they were fishermen. And he said to them, "Follow me, and I will make you fishers of men." Immediately they left their nets and followed him.

Matthew 4:18-20 ESV

Good Morning, Men of God!

Can we respond to the call of Christ the same way the first disciples did? In our text today, Jesus, who was becoming known in the region, called Peter and Andrew into service. Having heard the teaching of John the Baptist concerning Christ and having experienced His teaching and power (Luke 5:1-11), they had proof that Jesus was the chosen Messiah. They believed enough to immediately depart to follow Him in His work. It did not matter what they had built, or what their personal aspirations were. They had an opportunity to follow and know the Savior.

Can we follow Him and represent Him today with that same abandoned commitment? We, as Men of God, have seen and experienced the movement, miracles, and power of God. Everywhere we look we see evidence of His Sovereign Power in our lives and in the lives of those around us. He is calling us to follow Him in how we live and represent Him. Can we mimic the boldness of the first disciples?

This does not mean we walk away from our families and responsibilities. It means we hold our integrity as followers of Christ in higher priority than what this world says or thinks about us. It means we dedicate ourselves to the work that God is doing around us. It means we respond to the call of Christ in our lives daily. This does not take grand gestures. Can we just be determined to be in a place to be used by God? We need to be in a place of prayer and position to respond properly to our Savior as He calls us into His service in our everyday life.

Let us pray: *God, I love You. I am excited about the work You are doing around me every day. I am committed to following You and serving in whatever way You desire. Thank You for the privilege of being used by You. May the life I live give You glory! In Jesus Christ's name I pray, Amen!*

Love you guys,

Patrick

NOT THE UNDERDOG

And David said, "The Lord who delivered me from the paw of the lion and from the paw of the bear will deliver me from the hand of this Philistine." And Saul said to David, "Go, and the Lord be with you!"

1 Samuel 17:37 ESV

Good Morning, Men of God!

I heard a pastor break this down recently and I wanted to share it. David was not the underdog in the story of David and Goliath. Goliath and the army of Philistines were the underdogs. David had the army of the Lord and an experienced faith in God to stand on. He knew his victory in God was certain. Regardless of how big Goliath was, David knew who went with him into battle. He had already won!

As Men of God, our Father goes with us today. It is a certainty that some form of giant will try to intimidate us. Some situations will attempt to call us out of the Godly men we are. The same power that slayed Goliath will slay the obstacles in this day for you. The power of God was activated through

31

David by his faith.

I invite you to have faith in God and remember the victories He has already won through you. The power of God is activated in your life when you can recall past victories and use those memories to ignite your faith. The same Gracious, Loving God that delivered you last time, will do it again today. No Goliath will be able to stand in your way.

Let us pray: *Almighty God, my Father in Heaven. Thank You for the guaranteed victory. Please direct me as I take the boldness of David into every circumstance in this day. I know that You love me and that You are with me. Thank You, God. In Jesus Christ's name I pray, Amen.*

Love you guys,

Patrick

SPECTATOR OR VESSEL

As they were going along the road, someone said to him, "I will follow you wherever you go." And Jesus said to him, "Foxes have holes, and birds of the air have nests, but the Son of Man has nowhere to lay his head." To another he said, "Follow me." But he said, "Lord, let me first go and bury my father." And Jesus said to him, "Leave the dead to bury their own dead. But as for you, go and proclaim the kingdom of God." Yet another said, "I will follow you, Lord, but let me first say farewell to those at my home." Jesus said to him, "No one who puts his hand to the plow and looks back is fit for the kingdom of God."

Luke 9:57-62 ESV

Good Morning, Men of God!

Following Christ is the most difficult and rewarding job out there. Jesus doesn't care about your credentials, your degrees, or your previous experience. None of that matters to Him. He does not care about your sinful past. He died to redeem that. He only cares about one thing. Do you really want to follow Him? Being a follower of Christ dictates a willingness to walk the road He walked, even if it means experiencing some of the hardship He experienced.

In our text today, we see individuals pledging their allegiance to the cause before they knew what it would take. I am sure they saw the miracles and the growing crowds and wanted to be a part of the Jesus celebrity movement. Many are like that today. They want to see the spectacle of God moving but won't endure the sacrifice to be a part of the movement. We must decide if we are going to be a spectator, observing His mighty work around us, or a vessel used by HIM to perform these mighty works.

I believe as Men of God we find our true creation purpose in a position of submission as a willing vessel of God, willing to go and do the will of our Father wherever it takes us. Are you willing and ready to be used by Him today? I pray you will surrender further to His will and ask Him to use you. You are not a spectator! Get in the game and let God use you.

Let us pray: *Thank You God for the mighty works You are doing. Please use me today to accomplish Your will around me. I do not want to be a spectator. I am committed to being a part of the work. Lead me in the path of service You have called me to. My devotion is to You, Jesus. Thank You, Father. In Jesus Christ's name I pray, Amen.*

Love you guys,

Patrick

IN THE WORLD, NOT OF IT

For the time that is past suffices for doing what the Gentiles want to do, living in sensuality, passions, drunkenness, orgies, drinking parties, and lawless idolatry. With respect to this they are surprised when you do not join them in the same flood of debauchery, and they malign you; but they will give account to him who is ready to judge the living and the dead.

1 Peter 4:3-5 ESV

Good Morning, Men of God!

We should find very little similarity with the world. Look in the mirror! We are a royal priesthood, chosen Men of God. Whatever we do, say, watch, and listen to should tell a different story than our worldly counterparts. Our lives should reflect the Savior that was born into this world to die for us. After we have left the prayer closet and put the Bible down, our actions should still show our heart for Jesus Christ.

Our text today shows us that we make a statement when we don't take part in worldly outlets. It is noticed that we are not drinking, or cussing, or participating in lewd behavior. It is easy, in the professional environment to get "sucked in". We must resist. We will all have to give account for our life on earth. Let's honor God with our devotion to His will and character. We give others the strength to live for God when they see the unwavering standard we uphold. Remember, we are called to be in the world, not of it.

Let us pray: *Jesus, help me to take an accurate assessment of my life. I am called to be an example of You. Help me to firm up the Godly standard that You gave me. You have called me to be in this world as an ambassador of? You. I love You, Jesus. In Jesus Christ's name I pray, Amen!*

Love you guys,

Patrick

LET NOTHING TEAR YOU APART

But from the beginning of creation, 'God made them male and female.' 'Therefore, a man shall leave his father and mother and hold fast to his wife, and the two shall become one flesh.' So, they are no longer two but one flesh. What therefore God has joined together, let not man separate."

Mark 10:6-9 ESV

Good Morning, Men of God!

Protecting our wives goes beyond physically preventing harm or danger. There are many attacks on the Godly marriage that are intangible. We are called to protect our wives and marriage regardless of the adversary. Our text today shows us clearly that no man is to separate what God has united. We must be vigilant as Godly guardians over our most precious partners. That means anything that we do, watch, or say that can be a foothold of Satan to damage our union needs to be removed.

The rated "R" movie that you like, cut it out. The images that promote sexual promiscuity and violence, put them away. The time you spend with the fellas, monitor it. You need guy time, but intimate time with your better half is crucial to spiritual growth and marital confidence. When was the last time you used your words to admonish, encourage, and compliment your wife? If the answer is not "just yesterday", then it has been too long. Godly marriage is hard. Over 50% of Christian marriages end in divorce. Satan is working hard. You need to work harder. Desire your union today with your spouse, more than Satan wants your separation. Make the sacrifice. Put in the work. Let nothing tear you apart.

Let us pray: *Father God, please guide me in safeguarding the marriage you have blessed me with. My wife is my greatest companion. Guide me in protecting her vulnerable areas. Use me to stand against Satan as he desires to tear us apart. Show me how to love and protect her in a way that honors You. Thank You for bringing us together as one. In Jesus Christ's name I pray, Amen.*

Love you guys,

Patrick

PRAYER AS THE FIRST DEFENSE

Be sober-minded; be watchful. Your adversary the devil prowls around like a roaring lion, seeking someone to devour. Resist him, firm in your faith, knowing that the same kinds of suffering are being experienced by your brotherhood throughout the world. And after you have suffered a little while, the God of all grace, who has called you to his eternal glory in Christ, will himself restore, confirm, strengthen, and establish you. To him be the dominion forever and ever. Amen.

1 Peter 5:8-11 ESV

Good Morning, Men of God!

Keisha and I found ourselves in a heated discussion over an important matter. We were both passionately presenting our separate points of view. The tension in the room was palpable as tempers began to rise. Then, all of a sudden, I realized that we were saying the same thing. We had been arguing for multiple days over an issue that we agreed on. There just had not been enough communication about it to see the similarities in both of our viewpoints. In the end, it made me laugh. Satan is so clever.

Our text today shows us that Satan (the adversary) is searching for ways to tear us and our Godly relationships down. We are all fighting the same battle. Take heart in knowing that every man is fighting to maintain a happy marriage and relationships with his kids. Satan is attacking us all. He will not be victorious with any of us! God will restore, strengthen, and establish us if we keep seeking Him. I challenge you today to lead your wife or kids in prayer the next time a heated discussion arises. Glorify God as sovereign right during the situation. Watch how it puts Satan at bay and restores balance in your relationships.

Let us pray: *Thank You, God, for the gift of prayer. The ability to approach the throne of grace with humility is an awe-inspiring benefit of being Your child. Thank You! Open up my eyes so that I can perceive the attack of Satan on my marriage and personal relationships. Guide us to prayer, as we position You as Sovereign over every situation. God, You are excellent in all Your ways. Thank You! In Jesus Christ's name I pray, Amen!*

Love you guys,

Patrick

SECURE IN HIS BLOOD

He entered once for all into the holy places, not by means of the blood of goats and calves but by means of his own blood, thus securing an eternal redemption.

Hebrews 9:12 ESV

Good Morning, Men of God!

You have a reason to be excited today. It does not matter what day of the week it is. Jesus still sacrificed himself for your redemption. It was the perfect act of love, the ultimate display of sacrifice. This should cause you to enter every day of the week with rejoicing. If He was willing to sacrifice himself for you, what will he withhold from you today? If He was willing to endure agonizing pain for you, what will He allow to overtake you? If He died and rose to ensure your salvation, what will He allow to defeat you?

The answer to all three of these questions is the same: *nothing*. He did not secure us with the blood of animals, but with His own blood. In Christ, you already have the victory in this day and week. Walk out of your house today with the confidence of security in Christ by HIS blood. Enjoy your great, victorious day.

Let us pray: *Thank You, God, for the ultimate statement of love. Thank You for seeing the best in me and being willing to sacrifice Yourself. Today, guide me in walking in the victory that Your blood ensured. I will win, only because You have already won for me. Thank You for loving me! In Jesus Christ's name I pray, Amen.*

Love you guys,

Patrick

BIG SECRET

And he will swallow up on this mountain the covering that is cast over all peoples, the veil that is spread over all nations. He will swallow up death forever; and the Lord God will wipe away tears from all faces, and the reproach of his people he will take away from all the earth, for the Lord has spoken.

Isaiah 25:7-8 ESV

Good Morning, Men of God!

There is something that Satan does not want you to know: a secret that is a game-changer if you realize it. Satan understands that the end to his effectiveness starts with this realization. He fights against you with all his dark powers to distract you from this. There are potholes and obstacles thrown into your life to trip you up, just to keep you from fixing your eyes on this truth. What is this secret?

It is not really a secret. It is proclaimed all through scripture. It just takes reading it and believing it. Are you ready, Men of God, for the secret?

The Creator of the Universe is FOR you!

In the text today, it shows God taking away the power of death and wiping the tears of all His people. He takes away your shame and restores you. He redeems you. He is for you. You will go through a lot of stuff trying to lead your family. Today, walk in the realization that God is with you. It is simple, but it is often overlooked. In your decision-making and everything you do, know that God is with you or wants to be with you. You only need to ask Him. Don't allow Satan to distract you from the available unity with Christ. Put in the work this morning in prayer, reading, and meditation to make the connection to the Father. He wants to wipe your tears too.

Let us pray: *I love You, Father. Thank You for taking away all of our sin and pain. I praise You for Your consistent devotion to me. You are always on my side. Thank You for that. I surrender to Your will for me in this day. Thank You, Lord. In Jesus Christ's name I pray, Amen.*

Love you guys,

Patrick

GOD'S PROMISE

*By faith Abraham, when he was tested, offered up Isaac, and he
who had received the promises was in the act of offering up his
only son, of whom it was said, "Through Isaac shall your
offspring be named."*

Hebrews 11:17-18 ESV

Good Morning, Men of God!

Abraham is the Father of Faith. He was promised by God to
be the patriarch of a generation. As an old man, past years of
reproduction, he must have thought God got it wrong. How
could he, at 75 years plus, produce a child? Then, Isaac
became the proof of God's promise. He was the confirmation
that Abraham's ear was tuned to God's voice, the seed that
would become a nation, Abraham's pride and joy. God's
promise.

Then, God requested the sacrifice of His promise. God tested
Abraham to see if he would sacrifice his most prized
possession. Abraham believed God's promise beyond his

45

situation. Believing in God is the beginning of life for a believer. As Men of God, we should be in study of God's word to look for and understand HIS promises. When we know what God's word says, we can stand in the firm foundation of His promises, just like Abraham did. Take time today to read a few of these promises. Believe them and stand on them.

2 Peter 1:4 (NLT) And because of his glory and excellence, he has given us great and precious promises. These are the promises that enable you to share his divine nature and escape the world's corruption caused by human desires.

Jeremiah 29:11 (NLT) For I know the plans I have for you," says the Lord. "They are plans for good and not for disaster, to give you a future and a hope.

Matthew 11:28-29 (NLT) Then Jesus said, "Come to me, all of you who are weary and carry heavy burdens, and I will give you rest. Take my yoke upon you. Let me teach you, because I am humble and gentle at heart, and you will find rest for your souls."

Isaiah 40:29-31 (NLT)
He gives power to the weak and strength to the powerless.
Even youths will become weak and tired,

and young men will fall in exhaustion.

But those who trust in the Lord will find new strength.

They will soar high on wings like eagles.

They will run and not grow weary.

They will walk and not faint.

Philippians 4:19 (NLT) And this same God who takes care of me will supply all your needs from his glorious riches, which have been given to us in Christ Jesus.

Romans 8:37-39 (NLT) No, despite all these things, overwhelming victory is ours through Christ, who loved us. And I am convinced that nothing can ever separate us from God's love. Neither death nor life, neither angels nor demons, neither our fears for today nor our worries about tomorrow—not even the powers of hell can separate us from God's love. No power in the sky above or in the earth below—indeed, nothing in all creation will ever be able to separate us from the love of God that is revealed in Christ Jesus our Lord.

Proverbs 1:33 (NLT) But all who listen to me will live in peace, untroubled by fear of harm."

John 14:27 (NLT) "I am leaving you with a gift—peace of mind and heart. And the peace I give is a gift the world cannot give. So, don't be troubled or afraid.

Romans 10:9 (NLT) If you confess with your mouth that Jesus is Lord and believe in your heart that God raised him from the dead, you will be saved.

Romans 6:23 (NLT) For the wages of sin is death, but the free gift of God is eternal life through Christ Jesus our Lord.

The promises of God are powerful and awesome to grasp. I pray that these scriptures about God's promises were helpful to you today.

Let us pray: *God, I thank You for Your many promises. Help me to know them intimately. Help me to find strength in Your word. Thank You that You always keep Your word, and walk in Your promise. I Love You! In Jesus Christ's name I pray, Amen.*

Love you guys,

Patrick

PRIORITIES

"All things are lawful," but not all things are helpful. "All things are lawful," but not all things build up.

1 Corinthians 10:23 ESV

Good Morning, Men of God!

There is nothing wrong with having a hobby. I think that with the stresses we deal with daily, we need something to help us unplug. Every man needs an escape to unplug and reset for a moment. Just don't get lost in that pastime. Don't allow the hobby to consume you.

Our text today shows that all things are lawful, but not all things build up. There is a lot you can do that is not sin, but that does not mean you need to do it. It is OK to lower your sword for a quick rest, but don't be lulled by the enemy into never picking it back up. Enjoy a hobby but keep it in the right rank of priority. Remember, your loved ones require your attention. Your responsibilities as a Man of God have not left you. I encourage you to take your time. We all need it. Just make sure you are not neglecting responsibilities to do so.

Let us pray: *God, You have welcomed me into a Royal Priesthood. Please guide me as an ambassador to this world. As I engage in daily activities and hobbies, please don't let me get lost. Guide me in upholding Godly standards and priorities. Thank You, Lord. In Jesus Christ's name I pray, Amen.*

Love you guys,

Patrick

DEEDS OF THE LORD

They have lyre and harp, tambourine and flute and wine at their feasts, but they do not regard the deeds of the Lord or see the work of his hands. Therefore, my people go into exile for lack of knowledge; their honored men go hungry, and their multitude is parched with thirst.

Isaiah 5:12-13 ESV

Good Morning, Men of God!

We are very blessed. Even if there are things we would like to have, we are still more fortunate than 90% of the world's population. God has given us a lot. He did not stop with the ultimate sacrifice. He did not stop with the propitiation of our sins. No, every day He showers us with His grace and mercy.

The people of God in our text were experiencing God's favor. But once life got good, they forgot about God. They became so wrapped up in the provision that they overlooked the provider. That eventually caused their exile. They called on Him in bondage but forgot about Him once delivered. They knew how to access His presence and power when in need but forgot it once out of urgent situations. Today, be filled with knowledge! Know that it is God who provides, He who sustains. As we continue to exalt the Father, He will continue to bless us. I challenge you today to thank God not just for the obvious, but also the overlooked blessings in your life. He deserves gratitude for it all!

Let us pray: *God our Father, thank You for Your unending love and sacrifice. Help me to be conscious of my expressed thanksgiving and obedience in good times and not so good times. My circumstance will no longer dictate the frequency of my thanksgiving. Thank You, Lord! In Jesus Christ's name I pray, Amen.*

Love you guys,

Patrick

YOUR GIFTS

As each has received a gift, use it to serve one another, as good stewards of God's varied grace:

1 Peter 4:10 ESV

Good Morning, Men of God!

As Men of God, we share a few things in common. We are all called to service to God and His people. And we were all blessed with an individual gift that God has given us to help us better serve those in need. What is your gift? Are you using it to benefit yourself? Or are you using it to benefit God's people? If you look out into the community, you see a sea of need. If I look out, I see a sea of hurting people that have financial issues, mental issues, and physical issues, all manner of issues that need the gifting of the people of God to help them.

Our scripture today tells us that we each have an individual gift given to us to use in service to God and others. I am charging you today to examine yourself and identify your gift. Where does your gift fit in? Once you identify your gift, pray that God will show you how and where to use it to glorify His kingdom. If you already know your gift, get off your butt and go use it to glorify His name. If you know your gift and are using it to serve Jesus, To God be the Glory! Keep going!

Let us pray: *Thank You, God for Your natural gifting within me. Please illuminate it for me and show me how it can be used in my environment. Thank You for making me unique to serve you. Have Your way in this day, Lord. I love You! In Jesus Christ's name I pray, Amen.*

Love you guys,

Patrick

IN HIS PRESENCE

Where shall I go from your Spirit? Or where shall I flee from your presence? If I ascend to heaven, you are there! If I make my bed in Sheol, you are there! If I take the wings of the morning and dwell in the uttermost parts of the sea, even there your hand shall lead me, and your right hand shall hold me.

Psalms 139:7-10 ESV

Good Morning, Men of God!

There is no where we could go that the presence of God is not already there. As Men of God, we can see this as a good thing or a bad thing. On the bad side, it doesn't matter what sin we entangle ourselves in, God is always there. He sees His creation, who He loved enough to die for, not taking advantage of the opportunity of eternal life in Heaven and abundant life on earth. On the good side, it doesn't matter the hardships we go through, and it doesn't matter the circumstances in our lives. We have our Savior, who created the world and ensures that we breathe, right next to us every step of the way. So regardless of how alone Satan might want us to feel, we are never alone. God is always there. He's always there to hold us and guide us.

I challenge you today to take advantage of His omnipresence. Instead of feeling like you must make every decision yourself, seek His guidance. Pray His will, and pray blessings over your family continually throughout the entire day. Practicing existing continually in His presence leads to a closer relationship with God and stronger relationships in your family.

Let us pray: *God thank You for your omnipresence. You are everywhere, and I love it. Please guide me through every decision, and comfort me during the hard times. Please help me to live life with Your presence as a reminder of how to live. All glory belongs to You, God. Thank You, Lord. In Jesus Christ's name I pray, Amen.*

Love you guys,

Patrick

NO SURPRISES

But you must remember, beloved, the predictions of the apostles of our Lord Jesus Christ. They said to you, "In the last time there will be scoffers, following their own ungodly passions." It is these who cause divisions, worldly people, devoid of the Spirit. But you, beloved, building yourselves up in your most holy faith and praying in the Holy Spirit, keep yourselves in the love of God, waiting for the mercy of our Lord Jesus Christ that leads to eternal life.

Jude 1:17-21 ESV

Good Morning, Men of God!

The news has gotten depressing. When we turn on the radio or TV, we see death, destruction, and worldly pleasures. It is astonishing what our world has become. It really should not surprise us though. In the same way a meteorologist can look at the looming clouds and predict a storm, the mood of our nation and world was forecast in scripture. We should not be surprised. We should be ready!

If we read our scripture for today, I think we would agree it accurately describes the status of our environment. We must respond by keeping ourselves in God's love. That means we understand that He who created this world loves us and has not abandoned us. Regardless of the condition of our environment, God is still on the throne, and He loves You. Today, do your part to prepare yourself and your families to exist in this world. Make sure your children understand God loves them. Ensure you are contributing to the spiritual growth of your wife. Would you allow them to leave the house on a rainy day without an umbrella? Of course, you wouldn't! Don't let them go into this world spiritually unprepared.

Let us pray: *Father God, please guide me in preparing my family for the world we live in. It is dangerous and scary, but You are all powerful. Thank You for Your protection and love. Guide me in both setting an example of godliness and in leading my loved ones down the righteous path. I love You, Lord. In Jesus Christ's name I pray, Amen.*

Love you guys,

Patrick

HOUSE DIVIDED

But he, knowing their thoughts, said to them, "Every kingdom divided against itself is laid waste, and a divided household falls."

Luke 11:17 ESV

Good Morning, Men of God!

We have many friends in this world. Be it at work or at church, we find ourselves spending time with individuals that add value to us. This kind of fellowship is something that is positive and enriches the way we live. However, the most important relationships we have are the ones that reside in our household. Starting with our wives, it is important we take time to cultivate, build, and restore these relationships that help guard our hearts and our spiritual well-being.

Our scripture today shows us the house divided against itself cannot stand. We don't NEED to be on good terms with people outside of our home. It is, however, crucial to our lives and the lives of our loved ones that we live in peace and

Godly order with those who rely on us. That does not mean that we don't have disagreements or times of discrepancy. It just means that we allow the Holy Spirit to lead us towards fruitful relationships that foster spiritual accountability and growth in our household. If our house is divided, then we and those who depend on us will become easy prey for Satan. Lead with love.

Let us pray: *God, please bless my house with unity. Show me how to communicate love to my family in a way that is received and reciprocated. Please allow Your Holy Spirit to draw my family together in Godly love. I love You, Lord. In Jesus Christ's name I pray, Amen.*

Love you guys,

Patrick

UNBELIEF

Where your fathers put me to the test and saw my works for forty years. Therefore, I was provoked with that generation, and said, 'They always go astray in their heart; they have not known my ways.' As I swore in my wrath, 'They shall not enter my rest.'"

Hebrews 3:9-11 ESV

And to whom did he swear that they would not enter his rest, but to those who were disobedient? So, we see that they were unable to enter because of unbelief.

Hebrews 3:18-19 ESV

Good Morning, Men of God!

The battle of unbelief is something we all struggle with from time to time. We find ourselves in situations that seem too big, and we question whether God can be God in our situation. In those moments, we begin to experience unrest as anxiety, worry, and fear settle in. We end up in a situation devoid of the power of God, not because God is not able, but because of our lack of belief.

In our first text today, the writer references 40 years of miracles, and a people that still lived with characteristics of unbelief. The people of Israel were delivered from slavery and provided for in the wilderness for 40 years. They experienced the tangible, visible power of God daily, but they still doubted in their hearts. Are we different from them? We also experience God daily. His protection. His love. His provision. We bathe in it, daily, but how does it affect our belief? This is a question we all must answer individually. I pray that you apply what God has done for you in the past to your next crisis of belief. The same God that sustained you in the last storm will shelter you in the next. Trust Him.

Let us pray: *Thank You, Lord, for the many miracles You have performed in my life. The sheer provision that you shower on my family daily shows your power. Please guide me in using all of these situations to grow my belief going forward. As the enemy attacks, my experience with your greatness will propel me to new levels of belief and trust in You. Thank You, Lord. In Jesus Christ's name I pray, Amen.*

Love you guys,

Patrick

PRAISE BREAK!

For we ourselves were once foolish, disobedient, led astray, slaves to various passions and pleasures, passing our days in malice and envy, hated by others and hating one another. But when the goodness and loving kindness of God our Savior appeared, he saved us, not because of works done by us in righteousness, but according to his own mercy, by the washing of regeneration and renewal of the Holy Spirit, whom he poured out on us richly through Jesus Christ our Savior, so that being justified by his grace we might become heirs according to the hope of eternal life.

Titus 3:3-7 ESV

Good Morning, Men of God!

As much as possible, I like to take a praise break. A praise break is when you look yourself in the mirror and see how insufficient and unqualified you are without Jesus Christ. Then you remember that because of HIS sacrifice, you are whole and new in HIM. That deserves a shout!

Somewhere in the first few lines of our text today, you will find a description of your old self. You need to identify with that old person and use it as a catalyst to rejoice over your new creation in Christ Jesus, our Lord. He looked at you and saw through the facade, the lies, and the words. He saw your dirty, unworthy self, and He still died and rose for you. Hallelujah, Jesus! I encourage you to live for HIS glory today. Take a few minutes and just thank Him.

Let us pray: *Dear God, thank You for making me new every day. Thank You for taking the old me away and building a new me on the foundation of Your love, God. There is no way to live life fulfilled without You. Thank You that I don't have to do that. Bless Your name, Jesus. In Jesus Christ's name I pray, Amen.*

Love you guys,

Patrick

NO WORDS!

They profess to know God, but they deny him by their works.
They are detestable, disobedient, unfit for any good work.

Titus 1:16 ESV

Good Morning, Men of God!

What do your actions say? If your life over the past 6 months was muted, and all people were able to see were your actions, what would they say? Would your actions say you were a loving father, a sports enthusiast, or a hard worker? You can fill the world up by saying words that do not mean a thing. It is your actions that dictate what you truly believe.

In our text today, we see Paul describing a class of people called detestable in the eyes of God. Not the fleshly sinner, but the professing Christian without actions to support what he or she is professing. We must be willing to stand for Jesus and lead by word and deed. We all profess Jesus Christ as our personal Savior. We proclaim to put our faith in HIM! Therefore, at work, at home, and everywhere we go, our lives should support that proclamation. Notice that none of the above examples of what our actions would say about us are bad. Loving father, sports enthusiast, and hard worker are not bad descriptions. They only become bad when they are unbalanced. If Faithful Servant of God (or some form of this) does not lead the description, we need to reevaluate where we put our time and attention. I don't know about you, but I do not want my God in Heaven describing me as "detestable".

Let us pray: *God Almighty, please forgive me if my actions and words do not align. Help me to be sensitive today to what I show, and how it reflects You. Cleanse me from the inside out. Make me over in a way that the reflection of Your goodness bounces off of me and draws others to Your glory. Help me to be conscious of what I say and how I represent You. In Jesus Christ's name I pray, Amen.*

Love you guys,

Patrick

IMPORTANCE OF INTIMACY

Husbands, love your wives, as Christ loved the church and gave himself up for her, that he might sanctify her, having cleansed her by the washing of water with the word.

Ephesians 5:25-26 ESV

Fathers do not provoke your children to anger but bring them up in the discipline and instruction of the Lord.

Ephesians 6:4 ESV

Good Morning, Men of God!

The word 'intimate' means to have a close familiar relationship with someone or something. Our daily pursuit should be to have an intimate relationship with the Father. Through prayer, reading, and serving, our lives should be devoted to growing closer to him daily. But how is our intimacy with our family?

As fathers and husbands, those we lead desire an intimate relationship with us in a similar way that we desire it from the

Father. They want our time and attention. They want to feel our adoration and approval. They want to understand that they are important to us. We can accomplish this by being intentionally intimate with our wives and kids. Our two texts today show us that we are to love and cherish our wives like Christ loved the church and lovingly train our children in the Lord. Taking time to do these things will lead us to intentional intimacy. Go sit on your son's bed and talk sports. Do your daughters nails and laugh with her. Hold your wife longer than you have in years and tell her you love her. Taking intimacy seriously will improve your relationship and open doors of ministry in your home. Try it!

Let us pray: *God, thank You for the call to intimacy. Lead me in growing closer to my family. Help me to be a safe and healthy place for each of them. Help me to be vulnerable to them as I encourage them to be open to me. Thank You, Lord, for my loved ones. Live in our midst. In Jesus Christ's name I pray, Amen.*

Love you guys,

Patrick

FAILURE IS NOT AN OPTION

Not only that, but we rejoice in our sufferings, knowing that suffering produces endurance, and endurance produces character, and character produces hope, and hope does not put us to shame, because God's love has been poured into our hearts through the Holy Spirit who has been given to us.

Romans 5:3-5 ESV

Good Morning, Men of God!

"Failure is not an option" is a common phrase spoken in countless military or sports themed movies. If I were to transpose that phrase to apply to our roles as husbands and/or fathers it would read, "Failure is not an option, it is a certainty."

Doing this job well is a process, a daily pursuit of God's presence that will lead us to lead our families in the right direction. Sometimes, our failures or sufferings can drag us into depression and self-doubt. Our text today shows us that our sufferings and hardships work a process in us that will lead to a heart filled with the Joy of the Lord through His Holy Spirit. It is these tough situations, these perceived failures that, if we faint not, lead us to be the Men in God our wives and kids need us to be. Failure is a certainty because it is crucial to our success in Jesus Christ. It reminds us of our need and dependency on the Almighty God.

Let us pray: *Almighty God and Savior Jesus Christ, thank You for being perfect so I do not have to be. Please use my errors to teach me Your way. Draw me closer to You, Jesus, and guide my decisions. As I embrace my failures, help me to see them as opportunities for growth. Have Your way in me, God. In Jesus Christ's name I pray, Amen.*

Love you guys,

Patrick

BATTLE OF ANXIETY

*For you formed my inward parts; you knitted me together in my
mother's womb.*

Psalms 139:13 ESV

Good Morning, Men of God!

I never really battled with anxiety. I would hear peers talking
about it, but I never understood, until recently. It feels like
everything I know to be fact is being shaken. It is a
nervousness about the circumstances surrounding me that is
almost paralyzing. It is a very real and tangible battle. But as
real as it is, we, as Men of God, have no time for it. Living in
anxiety is contrary to belief in God as Sovereign Lord and
Ruler. I am not trying to be insensitive. I am speaking to
myself as much as to you.

The text today shows us that God knew us before we were
even conscious of our creation. He knitted us together. He
carefully created us. He is in control. Nothing surprises HIM.
If you are dealing with anxiety today, I encourage you to re-

center yourself. Understand that you are not in control. God is! Find comfort that He who knitted you together wants the best for HIS creation. Find comfort in HIS presence through prayer. Combat anxiety with the reality of God's Sovereignty in your life.

Let us pray: *Thank You for being in the driver's seat, Lord. I surrender to Your way and plan for my life. Help me to rely on You completely. I command that anxiety and worry in me will give way to faith and confidence in You. Thank You, Jesus, for being my healer, and removing all of my anxiety. I trust in You alone. In Jesus Christ's name I pray, Amen.*

Love you guys,

Patrick

PRAY ALWAYS!

I desire then that in every place the men should pray, lifting holy hands;

1 Timothy 2:8a ESV

Good Morning, Men of God!

It is important that men pray. The foundation of our families and the Church is our relationship with Jesus Christ. The most important way we open the line of communication with the Father is with his Son Jesus through prayer. In our text today, Paul is instructing Timothy to guide men to pray everywhere.

Not just at church, or at home, or in the car, but everywhere. We need to fill every aspect of our lives with the presence of the Highest God. We must set that example for our wives and children to do the same. Remember, they will do what we do. Praying draws us closer to God. It brings a calm to our situation. It connects us with the Father. It brings peace to our minds. We have the ability today to take every hurt, joy, obstacle, and victory to the Creator of all things. Don't waste that opportunity. Let us fill our kids' rooms, our bedrooms, our jobs, the gym, everywhere. Fill them all with prayers that honor God. In doing this, we position ourselves to grow in Christ and lead our families in growing in Christ.

Let us pray: *God thank You for the ability to pray. The ability to bring my burdens, concerns, joys, and celebrations to You is one of the best parts of our relationship. Please guide me in being an example to my family of having a consistent prayer relationship with You. I desire that they will grow in relationship through seeking You. Thank You, Lord Jesus. In Jesus Christ's name I pray, Amen.*

Love you guys,

Patrick

HOLE IN THE WALL (LITERALLY)

The waters closed in over me to take my life; the deep surrounded me; weeds were wrapped about my head at the roots of the mountains. I went down to the land whose bars closed upon me forever; yet you brought up my life from the pit, O Lord my God. When my life was fainting away, I remembered the Lord, and my prayer came to you, into your holy temple.

Jonah 2:5-7 ESV

Good Morning, Men of God!

Keisha would tell me every day, "you need to take some time to chill your head out". This was her way of telling me that I seemed a little more stressed or anxious than usual. Like clockwork, I would respond, "Nah, I am good." This went on for weeks until something happened. I punched a hole in a wall in our bedroom (pause for reaction). Mounting circumstances made me feel like I was drowning, and I could not see my way out. I kept how I felt bottled up inside because that is what "men do". So, in the heat of the moment, during a simple "conversation" with my wife, I put my fist through the wall.

I think, as men, we feel like this sometimes, like situations are drowning us and we can't catch our breath. Our text today shows us that, like Jonah, when we feel this way, our prayers are our way out. Our prayers reconnect us and submit our circumstances to God. Our prayers help us to receive his provision in our worst moments. Don't be like me and wait until the mounting frustration can seemingly only be expressed by punching a wall. When you feel it mounting, remember that our God is there to restore, refresh, and redeem you. Take time to chill and reset.

Let us pray: *Lord, please forgive me for any time that my frustrations get the best of me. Help me to stay anchored and centered in You. In times of mounting frustration, lead me to a place of peace and solitude deep in Your presence. Allow my emotions to be communicated in a constructive way. Thank You, Lord, for Your patience with me. In Jesus Christ's name I pray, Amen.*

Love you guys,

Patrick

MOST IMPORTANT ASSET

He answered, "Have you not read that he who created them from the beginning made them male and female, and said, 'Therefore a man shall leave his father and his mother and hold fast to his wife, and the two shall become one flesh'? So, they are no longer two but one flesh. What therefore God has joined together, let not man separate."

Matthew 19:4-6 ESV

Good Morning, Men of God!

My wife can make me so mad sometimes. She challenges me. She disagrees with me. But without her, I would have nobody to challenge and make me better. I would have nobody to disagree with me and help me to see different vantage points. As mad as she makes me sometimes, she is my best friend. For every hard time, there are several life-changing good times. You see, she is my other half; the person God created to walk with me through life.

God made man and woman to be one, to work together and

hold each other accountable. As husbands, we must lose this notion that marriage is supposed to be easy. Marriage is a process in which two people become one flesh and grow together to look more like Christ. That is a hard process! Our wives are our closest and most important assets. Treat them as such. Today, take time to appreciate the contribution your wife makes not just to your house, but to you as a man. Make sure you are contributing to her too! As your best asset, she needs to be replenished by you. If a vessel continues to pour without being refilled, soon it is empty. Let's do our job and be good stewards of our most valuable asset today.

Let us pray: *Dear God, thank You for the beautiful partner You have given me. Help me to surrender to her Godly purpose in my life. Help me to encourage and hold her accountable in the way she does for me. Two becoming one is a complicated process. It is a miracle that can only be performed by You. Please unify us into one flesh God, that we may serve You all the more. Thank You, Jesus, for Your Love. In Jesus Christ's name I pray, Amen!*

Love you guys,

Patrick

FLOPPY BABY

Those who know your name trust in you, for you, O Lord, do not abandon those who search for you.

Psalms 9:10 NLT

Good Morning, Men of God!

As some of you may know, our family welcomed our 6th baby to the Wheeler clan. Baby Benjamin was born October 16th, 2018 and evened the score: 3 boys and 3 girls. As exciting as his arrival was, there was a lot to be learned about myself in the process. When my son came into the world, he was limp. My heart sank as the nurses called the "Floppy Baby" code. People rushed into the room to work on him. My heart sank lower. Keisha and I had not been able to name our beautiful baby boy yet. And I immediately thought, "This is why we couldn't name him".

But then I snapped back and remembered that God was in charge. As much as I loved this little guy, God loved him more. So, I put aside my fear and began to speak to my son. At the sound of my voice, he perked up, regained his color, and began to breathe on rhythm. You see, the outcome of the story turning in my favor is not what makes this story great. It's the presence of God in my time of fear. He did not abandon me. With everything going on within His immense creation, He was present with me at Tampa General. So, I encourage you today to seek the Father and trust that regardless of the circumstances, He will NEVER abandon you. In your anxious, confused, or fearful moments, stop and breathe in His presence. He is there for you.

Let us pray: *God thank You for being true to Your word. You will never leave nor forsake us. Thank You for being present and tangible in our most troubled times. Please help us to immediately reject fear and to take hold of FAITH in scary situations. Thank You for loving and looking out for me. In Jesus Christ's name I pray, Amen*

Love you guys,

Patrick

WHATEVER YOU HAVE

Lifting up his eyes, then, and seeing that a large crowd was coming toward him, Jesus said to Philip, "Where are we to buy bread, so that these people may eat?" He said this to test him, for he himself knew what he would do. Philip answered him, "Two hundred denarii worth of bread would not be enough for each of them to get a little." One of his disciples, Andrew, Simon Peter's brother, said to him, "There is a boy here who has five barley loaves and two fish, but what are they for so many?" Jesus said, "Have the people sit down." Now there was much grass in the place. So, the men sat down, about five thousand in number. Jesus then took the loaves, and when he had given thanks, he distributed them to those who were seated. So also, the fish, as much as they wanted.... Whoever feeds on my flesh and drinks my blood has eternal life, and I will raise him up on the last day.

John 6:5-11, 54 ESV

Good Morning, Men of God!

We do not have an accurate view of the Kingdom needs around us. We see everything from a one-dimensional viewpoint. God sees the need and the provision for the need in the same line of sight. Our job is to surrender whatever we have, regardless of how little, to the Father for His use. A small amount of resources backed with the surrender and faithfulness of a believer goes a long way.

In John 6, we see Jesus feed over five thousand people with three fish and five loaves of bread. This amount of food was sufficient for one person outside of the hand of God. But in the hand of Jesus, this small amount became more than enough. I encourage you to be like the obedient young boy who surrendered his lunch. Don't see the size of the need and assess that your contribution can't bring change. Faithfully surrender your best to Jesus and watch him multiply and magnify your gift of time, talent, or tithe to meet the Kingdom needs around you.

Let us pray: *Father, I thank You for the heart to give. Whether it be time, talent, or tithe, thank You for using my gift to grow Your kingdom. Help me to focus less on amount, and more on my obedience to Your instruction. Whatever You require out of me is already Yours. Thank You, Jesus. In Jesus Christ's name I pray, Amen.*

Love you guys,

Patrick

MY BROTHER'S BURDEN

Share each other's burdens, and in this way obey the law of Christ.

Galatians 6:2 NLT

Good Morning, Men of God!

Each one of us understands the burdens that we deal with as fathers and husbands. Every day presents a new array of obstacles that try to stand in the way of us being Godly men. Our scripture this morning in Galatians 6 gives us direction to share each other's burdens. By doing this we demonstrate God's true instruction to us, and that is to love each other as we love ourselves.

Sharing a burden with a brother is a reciprocal action. Even though we may not be in need now, we can shoulder the burden of our brother. Then, when we are in need, there are people there to help shoulder our burdens. Recently we had one of our brothers reach out in need. Many felt led to help shoulder his burden. It was the love and sacrifice that eased the stress on our brother and his family. This week, keep your eyes open and pay attention to the people around you. It does not matter if it is prayer, or you are feeling led to physically help a situation. Be willing to help shoulder the burden of your fellow brothers.

Let us pray: *God, I thank You for my brothers in Christ. Please unite me with other Godly men ready to help shoulder each other's burdens. As men, we understand the struggle to hold the gold standard. Please strengthen us, Father, in your power. In Jesus Christ's name I pray, Amen.*

Love you guys,

Patrick

TOO COOL TO PRAISE!

And David danced before the Lord with all his might. And David
was wearing a linen ephod. So, David and all the house of Israel
brought up the ark of the Lord with shouting and with the sound
of the horn. As the ark of the Lord came into the city of David,
Michal the daughter of Saul looked out of the window and saw
King David leaping and dancing before the Lord, and she
despised him in her heart. And David said to Michal, "It was
before the Lord, who chose me above your father and above all his
house, to appoint me as prince over Israel, the people of the
Lord — and I will celebrate before the Lord. I will make myself yet
more contemptible than this, and I will be abased in your eyes.
But by the female servants of whom you have spoken, by them I
shall be held in honor."

2 Samuel 6:14-16, 21-22 ESV

Good Morning, Men of God!

We all have something to thank God for. Even if you are
dealing with struggles right now, the fact that you are reading
this means you are alive. That by itself is enough to sing

praises to God. In our text today, King David was so thankful, so overwhelmed by the presence of God that he danced his clothes off. Now, I am not telling you to get naked; but when was the last time you stopped to praise God with the same enthusiasm that you cheer for your favorite sports team?

Are you too cool to praise? I don't mean the quiet, mumble praise. I mean the outward HALLELUJAH cry that expresses your gratitude to the Risen Savior for dying for our sins. The leaping "GLORY, GOD!" that showcases your thankfulness for the provision for your family. If you do it for college football, do it for Jesus. There will be some people, like in the text, that don't understand your praise. That is fine. When they ask you about it, use that as an opportunity to share Jesus Christ. Even amidst adversity, there is a lot to thank God for. Don't be too cool to praise!

Let us pray: *My Lord and Ruler, you have done so much for me. Please forgive me if I ever acted "too cool to praise". Help me to freely express my gratitude at all times. You are my God and Ruler. Thank You! In Jesus Christ's name I pray, Amen!*

Love you guys,

Patrick

GOD-GIVEN GIFTS

A man's gift makes room for him and brings him before the great.

Proverbs 18:16 ESV

Good Morning, Men of God!

Don't lose hold of why God created you. What is that thing you do that gives you Godly joy? Don't get me wrong, I am blessed to have my 9 to 5. I enjoy it and it allows me to take care of my loved ones. God made me for something more. It is very easy to get lost in the daily ins and outs and forget about purpose.

Our text today shows us that it is our gifts, the Godly impartation of what makes us unique, that helps us carve a place in this world. It is our Godly purpose that gives us life. Inside each of us is a purpose that aligns with the gifts God has given us. These God-given gifts are our tools to living the abundant life that we were intended to live. As we begin a new week, I encourage you to remember your gifts, and allow

God to use them.

Let us pray: *God, please ignite the vision of every man reading these pages. Like Joseph, show them vivid dreams of why You created them. Highlight their gifts, and instruct them on how to glorify You with their gifts. Bless Your name, Jesus. In Jesus Christ's name I pray, Amen!*

Love you guys,

Patrick

FORGIVENESS OR CHANGE OF HEART?

If we confess our sins, he is faithful and just to forgive us our sins and to cleanse us from all unrighteousness.

1 John 1:9 ESV

Good Morning, Men of God!

Making mistakes is an everyday part of life. Regardless of who we are, we are going to make missteps that bring us to a place of needing forgiveness. Our scripture today shows us that God is willing and ready to forgive our sins and cleanse us of all unrighteousness if we just confess. The process of being forgiven is simple. Understanding whether it is truly forgiveness we need is more difficult. If we have a trait, or sin issue, that we consistently must repent for, then we must ask God to examine our hearts.

Psalm 139: 23-24 shows us an example of how to ask God to search our hearts. My encouragement to you today is to be willing to allow God to examine you. Look in the mirror and see yourself truthfully. If there is any sin issue, or item that you continually must ask for forgiveness for, give it to God. He already knows. He loves us anyway. Through confession, we can free ourselves and receive true forgiveness, and if needed, a change of heart.

Let us pray: *Almighty Savior and Ruler, please direct our hearts towards repentance. Reveal our sin to us in a way that is undeniable. Help us to stand in the mirror to allow You to show us who we are, and what parts of ourselves have to die in order to serve You. God, I love You. In Jesus Christ's name I pray, Amen!*

Love you guys,

Patrick

CAN I KEEP IT *REAL*?

When the enemy comes in like a flood, The Spirit of the Lord will lift up a standard against him.

Isaiah 59:19b NKJV

Good Morning, Men of God!

I must keep it real. This week has been one of the hardest weeks I have had since moving to Florida! Satan has been against me with every step. There were times where I felt like I could feel him trying to choke me out. As most of you might know, Keisha and I are in the final stages of planting Preservation Church. God has given us a vision for an outreach-based ministry focused on Welcoming All Wounded, Worshiping the Risen Savior, and Witnessing to a Lost World. He has called us to do this with a minimal financial footprint. This will allow us to reach and meet the spiritual and natural needs of the families and individuals in the Palm River/Clair Mel area of Tampa.

True to HIS promise, God has worked miracles to provide an awesome space, and we are moving closer to starting. It seems the closer we get, the more the enemy wars against us. This brought me to our text for the day. In Isaiah 59, it describes the enemy coming in like a flood. A flood is sudden and sweeping. You can't really prepare for it. It is swift and deadly. It does not trickle in slowly. One second you are good, the next you think you are drowning. But the text does not end there! It says that when – not if, but *when* – the enemy comes in like a powerful, unexpected, sweeping flood, the Spirit of the Lord will lift a standard against him. That standard is the anchor in the time of flood. It is our protection. It is the rooted Jesus Christ. If we hang on to HIM, the flood can be as strong as it wants. As we finish this week, pay less attention to the flood, and more attention to the standard that is His provision to get you through the flood. Why worry about rushing water when your standard WALKS ON IT!?

Let us pray: *God, nothing can defeat me as long as I am in You. Help me to find peace in the most complicated times because I rest in You. Thank You for seeing each and every one of our visions to completion. Please be our guiding light during the difficult times. In Jesus Christ's name I pray, Amen.*

Love you guys,

Patrick

OVERCOMING HARDSHIP

Have you not known? Have you not heard? The Lord is the everlasting God, the Creator of the ends of the earth. He does not faint or grow weary; his understanding is unsearchable. He gives power to the faint, and to him who has no might he increases strength.

Isaiah 40:28-29 ESV

Good Morning, Men of God!

The good days are easy! Your wife loves you. Your kids listen to you. Your job is good. Let's face it, we love life when everything is clicking. These are the days when it is easy to represent Jesus Christ. Someone asks us how our day is, and we preach for 5 minutes on the goodness of the Lord.

That is all wonderful, but what about the weak days? The days where the wife rolls her eyes. The kids ignore you, and you may be on the chopping block at work. Is God any less God? Is Jesus any less Savior? Not at all! In our text today, we see that God is understanding. He is ready with bountiful strength in times of weakness. He neither waivers, nor gets weary. He is constant and consistent. We always have a reason to praise and give testimony to HIS goodness. His provision is present on the good days and the days on which we are overcoming hardship.

Let us pray: *God help me to rejoice in You even during the bad days. Help me to realize that You are sovereign in both the sunshine and the rain. No matter the circumstance, You are Lord and Ruler. Guide me as I focus on You to overcome hardship. In Jesus Christ's name I pray, Amen.*

Love you guys,

Patrick

HAIL KING JESUS

And when Jesus had stepped out of the boat, immediately there met him out of the tombs a man with an unclean spirit. He lived among the tombs. And no one could bind him anymore, not even with a chain, for he had often been bound with shackles and chains, but he wrenched the chains apart, and he broke the shackles in pieces. No one had the strength to subdue him. Night and day among the tombs and on the mountains, he was always crying out and cutting himself with stones. And when he saw Jesus from afar, he ran and fell down before him.

Mark 5:2-6 ESV

Good Morning, Men of God!

Our way of dealing with obstacles in our lives can be backwards. When things arise, we often set out to make our plan and execute it to solve the problem. We use our wisdom, our experiences, and our strength to accomplish the task at hand. When challenges arise, and we address them like that, we are wrong.

If we look at our scripture today, the people attempted to subdue and "handle" the demon possessed man on numerous occasions. All their attempts failed. Then came Jesus Christ! The simple presence of Jesus calmed the possessed man, and HIS words cast out the demons. It works the same with the obstacles and challenges in our lives. Resist the temptation to "handle" the situation. Before you do anything, seek the Lord. Pray and ask God to guide you. Usher the presence of God into the situation and allow HIM to give guidance on how to handle it. We see our issues at eye level. He sees them through the eyes of eternity. I encourage you to honor God, even in knowing how to face challenges and obstacles.

Let us pray: *Thank You for being all powerful. I love You, Lord. Please guide me in seeking You first before I make decisions. Thank You for seeing my issues and already knowing the outcome. Worthy is the Lamb. Thank You, Lord. In Jesus Christ's name I pray, Amen.*

Love you guys,

Patrick

CHOICES EVERY DAY

I call heaven and earth to witness against you today, that I have set before you life and death, blessing and curse. Therefore, choose life, that you and your offspring may live, loving the Lord your God, obeying his voice and holding fast to him, for he is your life and length of days, that you may dwell in the land that the Lord swore to your fathers, to Abraham, to Isaac, and to Jacob, to give them."

Deuteronomy 30:19-20 ESV

Good Morning, Men of God!

The choices we make have a profound effect on the lives of our loved ones. With every decision or direction, we set an example for our children. In the scripture today, we are told to choose life, so our offspring may live. We have set before us every day the choice to trust God or not trust God. We have set before us the choice to live faithfully to the Father or not. We have set before us the choice to live a life that glorifies the Lord or to live a life that glorifies this world. All these are choices that have a direct effect on how our kids live their lives.

I encourage you to choose life and not death today. I encourage you to choose blessings and not curses today. Love the Lord your God and Creator. Understand that it is HE that gives you life, and HE that sustains you. And in Him you have length of days, prosperity, and peace. As you make that choice, your offspring will be encouraged to follow your lead.

Choose Life!

Let us pray: *Almighty God. Thank You for being a resource even in times of tough decisions. Please God, guide every thought. Please God, guide every action. Please God, guide every decision that I make. I understand that You know the path of my life and understand the best route for me to take. Help me to set aside my own desires, my own wishes. God, I know that Your way is so much better than my own. Thank You for being willing to guide me and to love me. In Jesus Christ's name I pray, Amen.*

Love you guys,

Patrick

SATAN'S SHORT GAME

And no wonder, for even Satan disguises himself as an angel of light.

2 Corinthians 11:14 ESV

Good Morning, Men of God!

Satan has an impressive short game. He is an aged foe that prowls, waiting for someone to devour. We all know the scripture. He comes to kill, steal, and destroy (John 10:10). He does not mount his attack on us in some elaborate, obvious scheme. Satan's attack on the Men of God is often subtle. Like our scripture says this morning, he disguises himself in a way that by the time we realize we have been tricked, it may be too late.

Thank God for Jesus! Regardless of how crafty Satan is, if we stay connected to the Father, HE will guide us around the attacks. He will give us Godly perception to discern situations and distance ourselves from sin. But like everything else, it takes effort on our behalf. God, our Father, is there to protect us. We must build that love relationship through prayer, studying the Bible, and submitting to God daily. If we allow Satan to devour us, we are allowing him to devour those we love. Most of us have some form of protection in our homes to guard against intruders. Worse than any worldly robber or thief is a thief that desires to steal the eternity of those we love. Let us find ourselves in prayer and submission today. Don't be fooled by Satan's short game.

Let us pray: *God, my Father in heaven, I know that Satan lurks, wanting to kill and steal my purpose, my promise, and my family. Please guide me around the attacks of the enemy. Open my eyes and my awareness that I may live a life that repels the enemy. Lead me in living a life above reproach, so that even when the enemy attacks, my faith remains that You will lift up a standard to protect me and my family against his pursuits. In Jesus Christ's name I pray, Amen.*

Love you guys,

Patrick

DON'T GET LOST

And Jesus came and said to them, "All authority in heaven and on earth has been given to me. Go therefore and make disciples of all nations, baptizing them in the name of the Father and of the Son and of the Holy Spirit, teaching them to observe all that I have commanded you. And behold, I am with you always, to the end of the age."

Matthew 28:18-20 ESV

Good Morning, Men of God!

The road of life has so many distractions. Even good things happening around us can draw our attention away from what is truly important. It is very easy to get lost in life. As believers we are called to make disciples. This is one of the last instructions Jesus Christ gave his followers before He ascended into heaven. When we allow the Holy Spirit to flow through us, we are led to situations and opportunities to share the Gospel of Jesus Christ.

Getting lost happens when we do not put in the work to make

ourselves available to be this vessel of discipleship. We get lost when we get content or even overwhelmed with life, and we fall out of daily communion with the Father. I encourage you today to remember your calling as a follower of Christ. Commit to putting in the time to fellowship with the Father daily. This closeness keeps you connected to HIS spirit. That connectivity allows you to be used and led by the Holy Spirit to follow the instructions of Matthew 28:18-20. Don't allow the duties of the day, or the "busyness" of life to cause you to forget why you are here. You are an ambassador of Christ, sent on this journey of life to make disciples for Jesus Christ. Don't get lost!

Let us pray: *Father, thank You for all the positive and productive things that you've allowed in my life. Your blessings continue to overwhelm me. As You are blessing me, please do not allow me to lose focus on the purpose of my creation. Keep in front of me the need to always make disciples to share Your love and to teach Your word. As a man of God, help me to take every opportunity I can to allow the light of Christ who lives on the inside of me to shine into the lives all around me. In Jesus Christ's name I pray, Amen.*

Love you guys,

Patrick

MEETING THE NEED

And my God will supply every need of yours according to his riches in glory in Christ Jesus.

Philippians 4:19 ESV

Good Morning, Men of God!

There are needs all around us, from our wives, our kids, our jobs. In all directions there is something or someone pulling on us. As providers and protectors, we sometimes take on the responsibility to meet all these needs. That is noble, but also not biblical. Our text today shows us that God supplies all our needs. Not just ours, but the needs of our loved ones as well. Sure, He may use us as a vessel to meet the need, but that is HIS choice. Our position should always be one of prayer and surrender. God will meet the needs of those around us however He wishes.

Focusing on meeting the needs of every situation leads to being overworked, anxious, and stressed. We are not built to handle such pressure. When we focus on Jesus, and fix our eyes on HIM, He will lead our efforts to the appropriate needs. Trying to accomplish everything always means we accomplish nothing, all the time. Today, I encourage you to step your "Prayer Game" up. Allow the Creator to guide your efforts. Fostering a loving prayer relationship with the Father is the beginning of hearing his voice and following his directions.

Let us pray: *Lord, thank You for our natural desire to provide for our families. As we work hard to do our duties, please allow us always to be reminded that it is You who provides. Help me to rely not on the job or the paycheck, but on You. And that in everything that I do I give You all the glory, honor, and all the praise. You are my true provision. In Jesus Christ's name I pray, Amen.*

Love you guys,

Patrick

GUARD YOUR HEART

The heart is deceitful above all things, and desperately sick; who can understand it? "I the Lord search the heart and test the mind, to give every man according to his ways, according to the fruit of his deeds."

Jeremiah 17:9-10 ESV

Do not be anxious about anything, but in everything by prayer and supplication with thanksgiving let your requests be made known to God. And the peace of God, which surpasses all understanding, will guard your hearts and your minds in Christ Jesus.

Philippians 4:6-7 ESV

Good Morning, Men of God!

In human anatomy, the heart is the core of our life force. It is such an important part of God's creative power in us. Someone can be "brain dead" and still be alive, but if the heart is dead, then there is nothing naturally that medicine can do to keep an individual living. In the text today, we learn that through prayer, supplication, and thanksgiving, the Peace of God will guard our hearts and minds in Christ Jesus. Why has

God in creation and scripture put such a focus on the heart? The answer is simple. The heart is the pumping life force in our bodies both spiritually and physically. If our hearts are corrupt, then we are corrupt. If our hearts are pure, then we are pure. Our hearts need guarding and spiritual centering because it is through the output of our hearts that we are judged.

The condition of our spiritual hearts has implications toward how God will use us. We are implored to rest peacefully without anxiety; but to pray, submit, and thank God continually for what He has already done, and what He will do for us and our families. Through this, God's peace will filter all those things out of our hearts that are contrary to a life of faith in God. Through continually praying, submitting, and thanking God, HIS peace will GUARD OUR HEARTS.

Let us pray: *God, please help me to understand the importance of the state of my heart. Lead me in guarding it, that I may be greatly used by You, Father. I love You, Father, and desire to have a pure heart focused on You. In Jesus Christ's name I pray, Amen.*

Love you guys,

Patrick

HEAVY BURDENS

Be watchful, stand firm in the faith, act like men, be strong. Let all that you do be done in love.

1 Corinthians 16:13-14 ESV

Good Morning, Men of God!

Being a husband, father, son, and/or brother are all hard jobs. We serve as protector, lover, helper, and anything else that those within our homes need. The spiritual, physical, and economic direction of our families sits at our feet. It can all be overwhelming sometimes. We are called to be peacemakers through loving our wives and admonishing our children. There is so much responsibility that comes with our roles in life. If I am not careful, I can begin to feel overwhelmed, and even a little down on myself. Then something happens.... I WAKE UP AND STOP BEING SOFT! Yes, it is a lot. Yes, it can be stressful! God did not form you by accident. He made us each warriors and protectors empowered by HIS direction, fueled with faith, and driven by His Holy Spirit.

The text today tells us to stand firm in faith, act like men, and be strong! This does not mean that we don't make mistakes. This means that we do not try to shoulder the burden of our role alone. 1 Peter 5:7 tells us to cast our burdens on the Lord. Are you doing that? I encourage you each to take a survey of yourself today. Do you feel stressed? Are you always worried? Is anxiety ever present in your life? If you answered yes to any of these questions, I encourage you to draw closer to HIM today. MAN UP and understand that your shoulders were not meant to carry the burden. You are His vessel. His power at work in you makes your calling possible. Without HIM, the task is impossible.

Let us pray: *Father, I thank You for the calling on my life. Being a Godly man is such a mighty task. Thank You for equipping me to perform the task. Help me to remember to rely on You in both tough and easy times. There is never a time where I don't need Your guidance and strengthening. Guide me in "manning up" and owning my role today. In Jesus Christ's name I pray, Amen.*

Love you guys,

Patrick

GUARANTEED MISTAKES

The steps of a man are established by the Lord, when he delights in his way; though he falls, he shall not be cast headlong, for the Lord upholds his hand.

Psalms 37:23-24 ESV

Good Morning, Men of God!

If earthly perfection was possible, we would have no need for Jesus Christ. Without Jesus Christ, it is impossible to grow to be more like God. We, as fathers and husbands, must accept that we are going to miss the mark at times. Even with our best efforts, we will still occasionally make a mess of situations. Thank God for Jesus!

The text today is a reminder that our steps are secured by the Father. Even if we fall, we shall not be "cast headlong", or thrown down. The only question is are we delighting ourselves in HIS way? Are we, with our time, talent, and tithe making his plan for us a priority? We have some responsibility in it. Our steps are established, but the security of knowing that even if we make mistakes God has covered them is dependent on our personal walk with God. It is not automatic. The security of this promise is based on our heart's desire to seek, know, and follow God. The course we navigate to lead our families is too crucial to rely on our own plan and intuition. Delight in the Lord today and live with the security that as we are leading, even if we make a wrong turn, HE will put us safely back on course.

Let us pray: *Thank You Lord, for knowing our mistakes before we make them. Guide me in seeking Your plan and not my own. Lead me in the way of the steps You established for me. Thank You, Lord. In Jesus Christ's name I pray, Amen.*

Love you guys,

Patrick

CAN'T PLEASE BOTH GOD AND MAN

For am I now seeking the approval of man, or of God? Or am I trying to please man? If I were still trying to please man, I would not be a servant of Christ.

Galatians 1:10 ESV

Good Morning, Men of God!

It is hard to maintain relationships. We want our wife to be happy with us, along with our kids, our friends, our coworkers. In a perfect world everyone that we interact with daily would be pleased with everything we do or say. We are unable to cover every base. We let some people down. We come up short on various occasions. As men with the desire to complete tasks and succeed in everything, that can be disheartening.

There is only one relationship that we should be supremely concerned with. Only one "person" we need to please. That is

God, the Creator of all! He that came in the form of His Son Jesus Christ to die for our sins. We NEED Him to be pleased with us. Whether or not we please Him has eternal implications for ourselves and those around us. As we put God first, and seek HIM as the priority, He will guide us in maintaining and developing external relationships. Don't over think it! The first step to pleasing God is spending more time with Him. Find time today to pray more, read more, or serve more. In doing that, God is pleased!

Let us pray: *Lord, my focus is on pleasing You. Guide me as I prioritize my time so that I can spend more time with You. Help me to make conscious choices that will lead me in a closer relationship with You. I love You, Lord. In Jesus Christ's name I pray, Amen.*

Love you guys,

Patrick

SEEK, TRUST, BELIEVE IN GOD!

Therefore, do not be anxious, saying, 'What shall we eat?' or 'What shall we drink?' or 'What shall we wear?' For the Gentiles seek after all these things, and your heavenly Father knows that you need them all. But seek first the kingdom of God and his righteousness, and all these things will be added to you. Therefore, do not be anxious about tomorrow, for tomorrow will be anxious for itself. Sufficient for the day is its own trouble.

Matthew 6:31-34 ESV

Good Morning, Men of God!

What are you seeking today? As men, our instinct is to pursue. We seek our wives, we seek success, we seek provision for our families. To seek is to chase after something with recognized priority. We spend the most time seeking what is most important to us.

In Matthew 6:31-34, Jesus Christ tells us that He knows our concerns and needs. We are not to be consumed with worldly seeking. God knows all of your needs and your family's needs today. Seek HIM as your priority today and trust Him to provide all your needs. We are called to believe in God for who He is. He sent His Son to save us. He has got your day in the palm of his hand. Through increased prayer, studying HIS word, and meditation, seek Him over anything else TODAY!

Let us pray: *God, thank You for the privilege of having a relationship with You. The priority of my pursuit will always be You. Help me to remember and live a life daily that sets You first. Thank You for already knowing what I need and providing for all of those needs. In Jesus Christ's name I pray, Amen.*

Love you guys,

Patrick

STAY AWAKE!

Clothe yourselves, all of you, with humility toward one another, for "God opposes the proud but gives grace to the humble." Humble yourselves, therefore, under the mighty hand of God so that at the proper time he may exalt you, casting all your anxieties on him, because he cares for you. Be sober-minded; be watchful. Your adversary the devil prowls around like a roaring lion, seeking someone to devour. Resist him, firm in your faith, knowing that the same kinds of suffering are being experienced by your brotherhood throughout the world.

1 Peter 5:5b-9 ESV

Good Morning, Men of God!

1 Peter 5:5b-9 offers a warning against pride. Today, let's be aware that it was only by the grace of God that we got this far, and only by His goodness that our loved ones are safe. The weekend is a fun time with our families, but no time to relax our spiritual seeking (Matthew 6:33). The same devil that was trying to disrupt your marriage and pollute your children on

Tuesday will still try on Saturday.

As the text instructs, let's continue to be aware of the attack. We are watchmen over those entrusted to us. The battle is not over. STAY AWAKE! The enemy is looking for you to drop your armor just a little. He wants you to pray less, read less, and love less. Regardless of what he tries, if you remain intentional, and resist him through seeking the Lord Jesus Christ, YOU WIN! Brothers, you are not alone. We are all fighting the same battles. God, our Father, will give us the collective victory if we remain steadfast in our faith. Have an overjoyed day!

Let us pray: *God, keep me alert to the attack of the enemy. Regardless of the day or time, let my focus be to cover my loved ones with prayer. You are our protection and covering. Thank You, Lord. In Jesus Christ's name I pray, Amen.*

Love you guys,

Patrick

TEMPTATION LURKING

*No temptation has overtaken you that is not common to man.
God is faithful, and he will not let you be tempted beyond your
ability, but with the temptation he will also provide the way of
escape, that you may be able to endure it.*

1 Corinthians 10:13 ESV

Good Morning, Men of God!

When we think of dealing with temptation, our minds easily
move to something related to sexuality. That is one form, but
there are many other forms of temptation. Any thought,
action, or situation that tries to pull us outside of God's will is
temptation. Regardless of what you are tempted with today,
God is faithful. In HIM you have already overcome. You may
be tempted to be dishonest, or to cut corners at work, or to not
spend the time with your family that you know you should.
Whatever the circumstances of temptation, Satan sends them
for one reason: to KILL YOU!!!

John 10:10 tells us Satan's desire is to kill, steal, and destroy. He wants to kill your purpose, steal your future in God, and destroy your family. Temptation is his method! God has made you GREAT. Greater is He that is in you than he that is in the world. Anything you are tempted with today, you already have the fortitude in the Father to overcome. Submit to Him. Seek Him for guidance. He will see you through safely.

Let us pray: *God help me to live outside of temptation today. Guide me in seeing the areas of my life that are vulnerable to temptation, so that I can further surrender it to You. Regardless of the source or focus, I lay all temptation on the altar today. I love You, Lord. In Jesus Christ's name I pray, Amen.*

Love you guys,

Patrick

MOST POWERFUL PROTECTOR

Trust in the Lord with all your heart, and do not lean on your own understanding. In all your ways acknowledge him, and he will make straight your paths.

Proverbs 3:5-6 ESV

Good Morning, Men of God!

Trusting our families in the hand of someone else is something that is not easy for us to do. We take seriously the job of provider and protector. If our families lack something, we make it our mission to fill that void. This is how we show our love. None of this is bad if we see it through the right lens.

Proverbs 3:5-6 compels us as men to put our trust in the Lord and lean not on our own understanding. We are to acknowledge (submit to) Him in every aspect of our lives, and He will direct our paths. This may be hard to swallow, but we have no ability to provide and protect. It is the Lord that accomplishes these things through us. As much as we love our families, He loves them more. As much as we want to give them, He has already given more. As Godly men, the best way we can take care of our families is to make sure we are having daily quiet prayer/reading time with the Lord. It is in these quiet moments that we submit to HIS HEADSHIP and learn how to trust the Lord. It is in these moments that He directs our path.

Let us pray: *God, thank You for making me a protector. I love my family and want the best for them. Help me to understand that my faith and trust can't be in my ability to protect but in You. You are the protector, and my trust is in You. I praise You, Father, for Your watchfulness over us. Thank You, Lord. In Jesus Christ's name I pray, Amen.*

Love you guys,

Patrick

TRUST THE PROCESS

For I know the plans I have for you, declares the Lord, plans for welfare and not for evil, to give you a future and a hope.

Jeremiah 29:11 ESV

Good Morning, Men of God!

Jeremiah 29:11 is often read without reading the previous 10 verses. In order to fully feel verse 11 concerning God's great plan for our future, we need to understand what comes before. In this chapter, verses 1-10 tell the Jews in captivity to settle in. It tells them to build houses, and to grow their families and possessions while in captivity. It implores them to endure the process. There is no quick solution. As men, sometimes we find ourselves in spots where there are no quick solutions. We don't want ourselves or our families to endure hard things. We feel like failures if we can't shield our lives from hardship or the "captivity" that causes us to, like the Jews, be in situations that are hard.

We must understand that pressure creates diamonds and fire refines gold. Wherever you are today, embrace your situation. Seek (there's that word again) the Lord for the learning moment in your situation. Allow God to make you the masterpiece He desires to make you. He knows what He is doing. The difficult nature of our situations does not make Him any less GOD! He has a plan and a future for us all! Trust in HIM who is worthy of our TRUST!

Let us pray: *God, my Father in Heaven, the process can sometimes be very hard. Waiting on change or a new situation is so difficult. Bless me with patience so that I can endure the process. Your ways are better than mine. Thank You for having a plan for me. In Jesus Christ's name I pray, Amen.*

Love you guys,

Patrick

PURPOSE IN PRESERVATION

We are afflicted in every way, but not crushed; perplexed, but not driven to despair; persecuted, but not forsaken; struck down, but not destroyed;

2 Corinthians 4:8-9 ESV

Good Morning, Men of God!

There is a Godly Purpose in your preservation. 2 Corinthians 4:8-9 depicts a life for the believer where no matter the obstacle, we are preserved. In HIS power, we are still standing! When something is preserved it is set aside and protected for a specific purpose or use. Why has God preserved you? We have all been through situations that could've, and maybe should've taken us out. Why did God, in all HIS wisdom, preserve you? You have been afflicted, perplexed, struck down, and persecuted. But the power of God through Jesus Christ that lives on the inside of you has allowed you to not be defeated.

There is Godly Purpose in your preservation. I encourage you men, if you know what your Godly Purpose is, walk boldly in it today. If you are not sure why God has preserved you, that is ok. Make it your focus today to ask God this one question. "Why have you preserved me?" Don't waste another day either not knowing, or not walking in God's plan for you. Seek the purpose in your preservation!

Let us pray: *Thank You God for preserving me for a purpose. Help me to see the purpose of my preservation that I might serve You with the gifts You have given me. I love You, Lord. In Jesus Christ's name I pray, Amen.*

Love you guys,

Patrick

RELENTLESS PURSUIT

Only be very careful to observe the commandment and the law that Moses the servant of the Lord commanded you, to love the Lord your God, and to walk in all his ways and to keep his commandments and to cling to him and to serve him with all your heart and with all your soul."

Joshua 22:5 ESV

Good Morning, Men of God!

It is very easy to be "committed" or focused on the Father when things are not going well, or there is a difficulty in our lives. As believers, we know that when push comes to shove, we can turn to our Father in time of need. But where is our true commitment? In Joshua 22:1-5, the people of God have entered and taken hold of the promised land. Joshua sends the tribes that lived on the other side of the Jordan back to live in their inheritance. He cautions them to remain committed to the God that brought them out of slavery and into a good place. He tells them to remember to serve and cling to the

Lord with all their heart.

Many of us have been taken through hard times to a much better place. God has sustained us and continues to provide. The question for myself, and for you guys is: are we as committed to the Lord in the Promised Land as we were in Egypt? Does our pursuit of His will for our lives in freedom match what it was in captivity?

As we go into this day, let's be committed to pursue the Father with all our hearts. Regardless of the outcome of our day or the condition of our lives, whether in sunny season or rain, He is worthy of all we can give and more.

Let us pray: *Father, your presence is worth constant pursuit. Guide me in relentless pursuit of your plan, purpose, and provision for my life. Regardless of the mood of the day, Lord, I will seek you with all that I have. I love You. In Jesus Christ's name I pray, Amen.*

Love you guys,

Patrick

LET IT SHINE

"You are the light of the world. A city set on a hill cannot be hidden. Nor do people light a lamp and put it under a basket, but on a stand, and it gives light to all in the house. In the same way, let your light shine before others, so that they may see your good works and give glory to your Father who is in heaven."

Matthew 5:14-16 ESV

Good Morning, Men of God!

We are called to be the salt of the earth and the light in a dark place. The Light of Jesus Christ lives on the inside of each of us. It is not our responsibility to hide it, but to allow it to broadcast everywhere we go. But where do we start? As husbands and fathers, our light needs to first shine within the four walls of our home.

Our families need to be intimately informed about our love for Jesus Christ, and HIS role in our lives. How much easier will it be for your wife to submit to you, when she knows you submit to the Father daily? How much easier will it be for your kids to hold a Godly standard in school, when they know their dad holds a Godly standard at work? Think about it. I dare you to ask your wives and kids today to summarize you in 3 sentences. How much of it will be about your love relationship with Jesus Christ? As we continue this week, I want you to let your light shine to your loved ones. You never know, it may give them the strength to let their own light SHINE for JESUS CHRIST.

Let us pray: *Lord, thank You for the light that You put on the inside of me. Your love shines through me so brilliantly. Help me to shine in my home first, that my loved ones know of my intimate relationship with You. Bless Your Name, Jesus. In Jesus Christ's name I pray, Amen.*

Love you guys,

Patrick

ETERNITY MINDSET

But recall the former days when, after you were enlightened, you endured a hard struggle with sufferings. Therefore, do not throw away your confidence, which has a great reward. For you have need of endurance, so that when you have done the will of God you may receive what is promised.

Hebrews 10:32, 35-36 ESV

Good Morning, Men of God!

It can sometimes be hard to live a life focused on Jesus Christ. Marriage, parenting, and working in a way that exudes a life of faith can come with many struggles. It takes endurance to always be Godly, peace-keeping husbands, understanding and doting fathers, and consistently confident providers. If we were to be "real" with ourselves, we would admit that it can all be a lot sometimes.

The text today calls us to remember the joy we felt when we were first enlightened, or came to the knowledge of Jesus Christ. We must remember that time and put our confidence in the Father. Everything we are doing is working towards the greatest reward: eternity with God our Father. Sometimes we need to remember why we started a journey, to give us the endurance to finish it. Today, remember why you gave your life to Christ, why you got married, why you became a parent, and why you are working. Embrace the struggle each situation can provide, knowing that you serve a God that has already given you the victory in each situation. Endure, knowing that at the end of this journey is an eternity in Glory with the Father. Use that eternity mindset to drive you today.

Let us pray: *My Lord and Savior. This life is hard. At times there are so many struggles. Please help me to remember the beginning. Help me to use the memory of why I started the journey to drive me to the finish. I pray Your strength will continue to sustain me. In Jesus Christ's name I pray, Amen.*

Love you guys,

Patrick

OUR CONDITIONING

Submit yourselves therefore to God. Resist the devil, and he will flee from you. Draw near to God, and he will draw near to you. Cleanse your hands, you sinners, and purify your hearts, you double-minded. Humble yourselves before the Lord, and he will exalt you.

James 4:7-8, 10 ESV

Good Morning, Men of God!

We are conditioned as men to "do the work". It is in our nature to make things happen. As manly and masculine as that sounds, it is not Godly. We have a Father willing to fight every battle and even exalt us in our humility. James 4 tells us to resist the devil and he will flee. We don't pick up a stick to beat him away, we don't walk into a situation saying, "I can handle this". We retreat into prayer, scripture, and accountability. This is how we draw near to God and humble ourselves to HIS power and will.

As we take the position of submission with the Father, the enemy MUST flee from us. Taking the prideful, "I got it" attitude can be damaging to us and those who are entrusted to us. As you go into the world today, there will certainly be obstacles and attacks. You don't have to fight the battle. PAUSE, PRAY, and PURSUE the Father in the moment of attack, or temptation. The power of God will be activated in your humility, and your faithful God will exalt you above the situation.

Let us pray: *Father, help me not to look into myself for the power to battle the enemy. As strong as I am, I can only battle and win in Your power. Help me to embrace the vulnerability of my weakness, so that I focus on retreating into Your presence. Thank You, Lord! In Jesus Christ's name I pray, Amen.*

Love you guys,

Patrick

LOVE EXPRESSIONS

But God shows his love for us in that while we were still sinners, Christ died for us.

Romans 5:8 ESV

Good Morning, Men of God!

We are called to demonstrate the love of God to all those around us. Love is the foundation of everything we trust and believe as followers of Christ. We are to pursue vigorously the example that Jesus Christ gave us. Romans 5:8 tells us that while we were yet (still) sinners, Christ died for us. Before we "showed good", before we loved HIM, before there was any tangible proof that there would be a "return on investment" for His perfect sacrifice, HE LOVED US.

He did not wait until things got better, or until we started doing things right. He poured out a perfect and complete offering to save our souls, no strings attached. As we have fun with our families today, let's strive to love in the same way.

Embrace and encourage those around us without looking for the same in return. Initiate the demonstration of patient, kind love in your home and environment. The beginning of those around us getting to know Christ better could be experiencing HIS love through us as husbands and fathers first.

Let us pray: *Thank You, Father, for loving me so purely. Today, help me love those around me based on Your example. Help me to be patient and kind. Lead me in embracing and encouraging my loved ones. Thank You, Lord. In Jesus Christ's name I pray, Amen.*

Love you guys,

Patrick

STEADFAST

Blessed is the man who trusts in the Lord, whose trust is the Lord. He is like a tree planted by water, that sends out its roots by the stream, and does not fear when heat comes, for its leaves remain green, and is not anxious in the year of drought, for it does not cease to bear fruit.

Jeremiah 17:7-8 ESV

Good Morning, Men of God!

Living steadfast lives with our trust firmly in the Lord is essential to being the husbands and fathers we desire to be. Being steadfast means to be unwavering regardless of conditions or opposition. This must be the main characteristic of our belief. The steadfast nature of our faith in God is fueled by our understanding that there is nobody on earth worthy of our trust, only God, only the Creator, only HE who was willing to die for us. This is the only place deserving of our hope and trust.

Jeremiah 17: 7-8 tells us that if we put our hope and trust in the Lord, we will be like a tree planted by water, not effected by turbulent conditions, but steadfast and fruitful regardless of the environment. I believe this consistency is what we all desire for ourselves and our families. That ability to be firmly planted, steadfast, and unmovable for our loved ones begins with where we place our trust. Anchor your hope and trust in Jesus Christ today.

Let us pray: *Father, please help me to be steadfast for my family. As the leader, the head of the house, they need to be able to count on the godliness in me. The only way I can be seen as trustworthy is through relying on You. You are my rock. My trust is in You. Help my family to trust the God in me. Thank You, Lord. In Jesus Christ's name I pray, Amen.*

Love you guys,

Patrick

EMBRACING CONTENTMENT

Keep your life free from love of money, and be content with what you have, for he has said, "I will never leave you nor forsake you."

Hebrews 13:5 ESV

Good Morning, Men of God!

It is easy to look around and see something that belongs to someone else and want it. As a father, maybe a friend of your child has a new car, and now you want to get one for your teenager. As a husband, maybe a coworker just purchased a new house for his wife, and now you want to do the same thing. It is very easy to fall into this trap.

Hebrews 13:5 calls for us to reject covetous behavior and embrace contentment. The text does not say we should be complacent, but content. This means to be satisfied with what God has provided, understanding that He knows our needs before they even become needs. The frame of our wants and desires must be that we have the best gift of all already. God will never leave or forsake us. Nothing is better than that. In a world that tells us and our loved ones that we need more, know that God is enough. Things are cool, but eternity with HIM is better! Let's keep eternity our focus today.

Let us pray: *God thank You for the many blessings You have provided. I honor You, Lord. Help me not to desire things that I see outside of my home. May I always walk with the understanding that You know what is best for me. The greatest gift anyone could ever have, You gave through Jesus Christ. Bless Your name, Jesus. In Jesus Christ's name I pray, Amen.*

Love you guys,

Patrick

POWER OF WORDS

Through him then let us continually offer up a sacrifice of praise
to God, that is, the fruit of lips that acknowledge his name.

Hebrews 13:15 ESV

Good Morning, Men of God!

In the book of Genesis, God spoke, and the world was created. When He created man, His word tells us that He made us in His own image (Gen 1:26). Proverbs 18:21a tells us that "death and life are in the power of the tongue." If we put these things together, we see that there is power in what we speak into the surrounding atmosphere. We can contribute to our environment just by what we say, be it positive or negative.

Hebrews 13:15 calls us to use our voices to lift praises to our God in Heaven. We have so much to be thankful for. Every breathe we take. Every step we take. Every time we hug one of our children. Every time we kiss our wives. Every moment deserves a praise of thanks. I know everything is not perfect for you. It is not perfect for any of us. God is still so deserving of ALL our praises. Psalm 22:3 tells us that God inhabits the praise of his people. What that means is that when we look beyond the everyday obstacles and continually submit praises to our Father in Heaven, we are welcoming HIM into our environment and situation. Sacrifice time today to thank God for the little things you normally take for granted. Fill your environment with Godly praises and watch how your day is filled with HIS presence.

Let us pray: *God, please guide us in using our words to bless and admonish, not tear down. May praise ring out from my lips all day long as I reflect on the overlooked goodness You provide every day. Thank You, Lord. I love You. In Jesus Christ's name I pray, Amen.*

Love you guys,

Patrick

NO ROOM FOR COMPLACENCY

"I know your works: you are neither cold nor hot. Would that you were either cold or hot! So, because you are lukewarm, and neither hot nor cold, I will spit you out of my mouth."

Revelation 3:15-16 ESV

Good Morning, Men of God!

Complacency has no purpose in the house of God. We are either on fire for the Lord and desiring to fulfill his Great Commission to go, teach, and baptize, or we have no understanding of who God is. Satan has convinced the church that it is ok to be lukewarm or complacent. He tells us that it is ok to simply come to church, give an offering, clap, sing and go home to the same sinful life.

It isn't ok. We are called as Men of God to draw a line in the sand and set a standard for how we love the Lord, worship Him, and serve His kingdom. God wants your very best. He deserves your very best. Don't let complacency get you. Start now refusing to be lukewarm. Get up and seek God to show you where He wants to use you and trust Him enough to be obedient to His direction.

Let us pray: *Almighty Father, please help me to keep charging forward in Your service. There is no place for complacency as we battle for souls as Your ambassadors. Show me where You would have me to serve. Light Your fire on the inside of me that I may serve with diligence. All to Your Glory. In Jesus Christ's name I pray, Amen.*

Love you guys,

Patrick

LIKE CHRIST LOVED THE CHURCH

Husbands, love your wives, as Christ loved the church and gave himself up for her, that he might sanctify her, having cleansed her by the washing of water with the word, so that he might present the church to himself in splendor, without spot or wrinkle or any such thing, that she might be holy and without blemish.

Ephesians 5:25-27 ESV

Good Morning, Men of God!

Our wives are biblically instructed to "submit" to us as husbands and heads of our houses. Ephesians 5:22-24 very clearly instructs that wives should submit to their husbands in all things. As men, we often stop reading after these verses. If we read a little further into the text for today, we see that great responsibility falls on us as husbands. We are called to love our wives like Christ loved the Church. Christ did not put conditions on His love. He did not say, I am only going to die for you if you listen to me. No, His love was not conditioned on anything the church did. Christ washed the Church with His word to sanctify (set apart) the church.

Are we walking in the example of Jesus Christ? Are we setting a foundation of love and spiritual unity with our wives? Are we "washing" or praying and reading God's word daily with our wives so that they may be cleansed and set apart? Before our wives can submit, we must be living a life as a husband that encourages them to do so. Christ demonstrated his undying love for the church before the church responded. Take time today, and every day, to pour spiritually into your spouse. Walk in love towards her, regardless of what she does. Exalt God in your relationship with your wife. We all struggle with this at times, but the scripture is clear in this matter. Loving our wives in God's way leads to better relationships and a stronger home.

Let us pray: *God, You have called me to love my wife in an extraordinary way. Help me to love her the way You love the Church. Guide me in taking my role as her spiritual head. Use me to exemplify Your love to her and my home at all times. Thank You for such a wonderful partner. In Jesus Christ's name I pray, Amen.*

Love you guys,

Patrick

GOD'S GUIDANCE

But the Helper, the Holy Spirit, whom the Father will send in my name, he will teach you all things and bring to your remembrance all that I have said to you.

John 14:26 ESV

Good Morning, Men of God!

One of the biggest fears for a father or husband is that he will inadvertently lead his family down the wrong path. We don't want to make a wrong decision that will cause years of damage to those who depend on us. If we allow it, this fear can affect how we show love and lead our families. Our Father promises that the Helper, the Holy Spirit, is here to teach us all things. We have no reason to FEAR wrong decisions. We need to tap into the Holy Spirit and receive Godly direction for our everyday lives. How do we "tap" into the Holy Spirit? It starts with prioritizing our love relationship with the Father. As we seek God first (Matthew 6: 33-34), we become more sensitive to HIS Spirit. As our ears are tuned to

HIS voice, we can receive the much-needed direction for our families. It all starts with where our priorities are.

How important is correctly leading your family to you? How much time do you spend in prayer, praise, and pursuing the Father daily? Don't pursue perfection. That is impossible. Pursue a love relationship with God our Father in heaven. Doing that will allow you to "tap" into the Holy Spirit and receive the help needed to appropriately lead your family. Make it a priority TODAY!

Let us pray: *Dear God, I don't want to lead my family in the wrong direction. Guide me in relying on the guidance of Your Spirit, and not my own sense of direction. Draw me closer to You that I may tap into Your Holy Spirit through a love relationship with You. I desire for my ear to be ever tuned to Your voice. Lead me, Lord. In Jesus Christ's name I pray, Amen.*

Love you guys,

Patrick

MUCH NEEDED REST

But he would withdraw to desolate places and pray.

Luke 5:16 ESV

Good Morning, Men of God!

The job of father and husband is a full-time job. We work all day, come home and work more, taking part in the management of our homes. It is in our nature to push ourselves continuously without regard for a break or resting point. In everything we do, our goal is to model our lives after Jesus Christ. In the Bible, there are several instances where Jesus withdrew away from the crowds, disciples, and responsibilities to devote himself to prayer. He took time to refuel Himself so He could continue to be of optimal use to the Kingdom of God and those He was ministering to.

In Luke 5: 1-15, we see Jesus preaching, calling disciples, and healing people. When we get to verse 16, we see that He took time to Himself to rest and refuel. Gents, make sure you are taking time to do the same. Wanting to work tirelessly for our families is honorable, but stupid. Without rest, or time to stop and pray to re-center ourselves with the Father, we put our ability to provide for and support those we love at risk.

Let us pray: *My Father in Heaven, help me to know when my "tank" is on empty. Resting so I can be ready for Your work is a good thing. Lead me in taking the example of Jesus Christ. Allow me to work diligently towards Your goals, and rest peacefully when needed. Help me to see that my exhaustion can be a tool of Satan as well. In Jesus Christ's name I pray, Amen.*

Love you guys,

Patrick

MY PLAN VS. GOD'S PLAN

Do not be anxious about anything, but in everything by prayer and supplication with thanksgiving let your requests be made known to God.

Philippians 4:6 ESV

Good Morning, Men of God!

A new season brings lots of excitement and planning. We get so concerned with wanting to start out strong and set the standard of God's best for our new season. We think about the mistakes of the last season, and we don't want to make them in this season. We convince ourselves that how we start this season will dictate how we end it.

Philippians 4:6 gives a very practical way of viewing this season. It is easy to get wrapped up in planning, goal setting, and organizing our attack plan. But the text calls us to prioritize prayer and supplication (to ask earnestly) in making our requests made known to God. Before you plan, schedule a meeting, or set something in motion, pray. Seek God for HIS plan for you. Don't inform HIM of your plan for yourself. Like sons to a loving Father, take your plans to God in prayer. Trust HIM, and rest in HIS planning and timing. Ephesians 3:20 says that God can do more than you can ask or even think. Whatever plan you have for yourself for this season pales in comparison to what HE has planned for you!

Let us pray: *Jesus, please forgive me for setting thoughts towards a plan without seeking You. Help me to live a life that seeks You to be informed of Your plan for me. Help me not to get wrapped up in the temptation to plan my steps based on what I see. My vision is limited Lord; Yours is infinite. Please give me Your plan, as it is always better for me. I love You, Lord. In Jesus Christ's name I pray, Amen.*

Love you guys,

Patrick

KNOW WHAT YOU KNOW

But in your hearts honor Christ the Lord as holy, always being prepared to make a defense to anyone who asks you for a reason for the hope that is in you; yet do it with gentleness and respect...

1 Peter 3:15 ESV

Good Morning, Men of God!

It is important to understand what we believe. As the spiritual heads of our homes, it is not enough to just say we believe in Jesus Christ. Why do we believe? What is our testimony? How can we convey the difference between the God we profess and the gods of other religions?

1 Peter 3:15 instructs us to honor Christ and defend our faith and our hope with gentleness. At first read, this scripture seems to direct our defense towards people outside of our home. If we think about it, the gentle defense of what we believe should happen at home, with our families first. As we

share stories of God's goodness, provision, and power in our lives, we will explain the reason for our hope. If we can make it a point to gently defend the reason for our hope in our home, our loved ones will be more equipped and comfortable defending their faith outside of the home.

Let us pray: *Help me to exude my faith in what I say and do. Guide me in sharing openly in my home the things You have done for me so that my family is driven to become familiar with what they believe. I desire for the intimacy that we share to be contagious to all those around me. In Jesus Christ's name I pray, Amen.*

Love you guys,

Patrick

WHAT DO I PURSUE?

The steps of a man are established by the Lord, when he delights in his way; though he falls, he shall not be cast headlong, for the Lord upholds his hand.

Psalm 37:23-24 ESV

Good Morning, Men of God!

The Lord honors our efforts. As our hearts are turned towards Him, and we set our true desire to do His will, we will still make mistakes. As the Holy Spirit is tuning our ears to His voice, we are certain to get it wrong sometimes.

Psalm 37:23-24 clearly shows us how the Lord upholds the righteous. It says that even though he falls, he shall not be cast headlong. God is not focused on our mistakes. He knows we are going to fall. He is focused on us helping us delight in HIS way. Don't pursue perfection; it is impossible. Pursue Jesus, and find joy in His plan for your life. In doing this, we make sure that even though we make mistakes that effect our families, our Father will not allow our mistakes to lead to destruction.

Let us pray: *God Almighty, thank You for this day that You have given me. Please forgive me for allowing the pursuit of perfection to be my goal. I will never be perfect. See me, as I pursue you. Bless our love relationship today. Through that relationship, please guide every decision and action today. In Jesus Christ's name I pray, Amen.*

Love you guys,

Patrick

FAMILY ARMOR

Finally, be strong in the Lord and in the strength of his might.
Put on the whole armor of God, that you may be able to stand
against the schemes of the devil. For we do not wrestle against
flesh and blood, but against the rulers, against the authorities,
against the cosmic powers over this present darkness, against the
spiritual forces of evil in the heavenly places. Therefore take up
the whole armor of God, that you may be able to withstand in the
evil day, and having done all, to stand firm.

Ephesians 6:10-13 ESV

Good Morning, Men of God!

Every single day we walk out of the door is a battle. As soon as we open our eyes in a new, God-given day, Satan is there to try to steal our purpose in God and discredit HIS work in us. Without the guidance of the Holy Spirit, and without putting on the whole armor of God, we would surely fail in the battle daily.

But we are not in the battle by ourselves. God has given us Godly wives and children that walk with us daily. Are we making sure that their armor is on? I believe we all understand the importance of seeking God in His holy word. Are we taking time daily to make sure that our families are prepared for the battle as well? The enemy is not just after you. He wants all those who belong to God. That includes everyone in your household. If you "win" the individual day spiritually, but Satan has his way with your family, you still lose. As Men of God, take time today to make sure that those around you are seeking God for their own love relationship. After you put on your armor, make sure that they are ready for battle as well.

Let us pray: *God, thank You for my family. Thank You for alerting us to the desire for the enemy to devour us. As I take hold of my armor today, please guide me in assuring that each member of my family is properly suited in their armor as well. I love You, Lord. In Jesus Christ's name I pray, Amen.*

Love you guys,

Patrick

ALWAYS REMEMBER

Then Joshua called the twelve men from the people of Israel,
whom he had appointed, a man from each tribe. And Joshua said
to them, "Pass on before the ark of the Lord your God into the
midst of the Jordan and take up each of you a stone upon his
shoulder, according to the number of the tribes of the people of
Israel, that this may be a sign among you. When your children
ask in time to come, 'What do those stones mean to you?' then
you shall tell them that the waters of the Jordan were cut off
before the ark of the covenant of the Lord. When it passed over
the Jordan, the waters of the Jordan were cut off. So, these stones
shall be to the people of Israel a memorial forever."

Joshua 4:4-7 ESV

Good Morning, Men of God!

Each day we face obstacles that seem insurmountable. Be it at work, church, or home, we engage in situations that challenge us and require more out of us than we have at the time. Whether or not we want to admit it, the possibility of defeat enters our minds and starts to grow roots. Joshua 4:4-7 shows the importance of remembering what God has already taken us through. This gives us the point of reference to believe that

God will take us through the next obstacle. The Israelites took up 12 stones from the Jordan as a memorial for generations to come, to remember what God did to preserve His people.

When we can remember what God did, we can remember who God is. This allows us to stand against any obstacles, because we remember that the same God that preserved us yesterday can do it today. Don't allow the weight, responsibilities, or obstacles of today to cause you to forget how God provided yesterday. Look to your own "12 stones", and believe that He is not finished doing miracles for you.

Let us pray: *God, My Father in Heaven, please help me to remember. You are an unchanging and consistent God. That means that if You preserved me the last time I was under attack, You will do the same this time, Lord. Guide me in recalling Your victories in my life, that they may keep me going to the next victory. Your works are mighty in my life, and in the lives of those around me. Direct me in using the memory of Your work to guide my footsteps forward. In Jesus Christ's name I pray, Amen.*

Love you guys,

Patrick

THE TRUTH IN TRANSPARENCY

Therefore, having put away falsehood, let each one of you speak the truth with his neighbor, for we are members one of another.

Ephesians 4:25 ESV

Good Morning, Men of God!

Being open and transparent with our feelings and struggles can be the most difficult part of being a man. My wife loves to go into model homes and get decorating ideas. It has never been my favorite thing. When she wanted to go this weekend, I shared with her that it sometimes gets me down when she gets these great, but sometimes expensive ideas, and we can't execute them when she wants. She is my wife. She deserves the world. It messes with me sometimes when we have financial constraints. In an instant, her whole view of the situation changed. She went from thinking that I "never want to do what she wants" to understanding more about me and my desire to see her happy.

Ephesians 4:25 calls us to put away falsehood and speak the truth to our neighbors as one body. This starts with the women God has given us to spend our lives with. As we shine truth into our marriage, we will see the level of intimacy increase as we invite our wives to know us better. Vulnerability to our spouses is not a sign of weakness. It shows that we love them and trust them with our inner most struggles. It shows them we are committed to a transparent life with them and encourages them to reciprocate the transparency.

Let us pray: *God, please open up the lines of communication in my marriage. Help me to drive to new depths of discussion with my spouse. Help me to see my vulnerability as a way to become more like one flesh with her. Guide me in opening up and evicting secrecy from my marriage. In Jesus Christ's name I pray, Amen.*

Love you guys,

Patrick

CAN'T BE LUKEWARM?

I know your works: you are neither cold nor hot. Would that you were either cold or hot! So, because you are lukewarm, and neither hot nor cold, I will spit you out of my mouth. For you say, I am rich, I have prospered, and I need nothing, not realizing that you are wretched, pitiable, poor, blind, and naked.

Revelation 3:15-17 ESV

Good Morning, Men of God!

The worth we bring into our families is not anchored in financial or physical security. The value we bring is based in the example of spiritual security we set. It is based in how our works echo the Kingdom of God and His purpose. Our loved ones are paying attention to where we stand as husbands and fathers. It is not enough to instruct them in the correct manner; our actions need to dictate our stance. We are either committed to the Lord and His work around us, or we are not. There is no room to be in the middle on our belief, how we live, and how we serve the Lord.

Setting a lukewarm example to our loved ones sets them up for potential failure. We can't afford to give the enemy that victory. Remember that they will do what we do, not what we say. If we make it okay to live a life of uncertain faith, they will follow that example. Let's set an example of *on fire* devotion to Jesus Christ that spills over into how we work, live, and love, every day.

Let us pray: *God forgive me if I am not living a life that makes my commitment to You plain. Help me to be aware of the example I am setting for my family. There is no room to even appear lukewarm. May Your fire burn deep inside of me for everyone to see. In Jesus Christ's name I pray, Amen.*

Love you guys,

Patrick

GOD'S STEADFAST LOVE

But you, O Lord, are a God merciful and gracious,
slow to anger and abounding in steadfast love and faithfulness.

Psalm 86:15 ESV

Good Morning, Men of God!

God abounds in not just love, but steadfast, immovable, unwavering love and faithfulness towards us. Therefore, we are called to a love relationship with HIM. The order of our daily pursuit begins with our walk with Jesus Christ, then flows to our wives and kids.

Today, respond to the most certain thing in your life with the appropriate attention. It's not like you deserve this steadfast, merciful love. It is the best gift you could ever receive as expressed through Jesus Christ. Don't "walk by" this gift today like the forgotten Christmas present that you purchased for your child. Respond to His unique, one-of-a-kind love with deliberate devotion and dedication.

Let us pray: *God, thank You for Your intentional love for me. Please forgive me for not responding to it with love and enthusiasm. You are my rock and gracious God. I love You! Thank You for showing me what steadfast love is. In Jesus Christ's name I pray, Amen.*

Love you guys,

Patrick

STANDING IN HIS STRENGTH

Submit yourselves therefore to God. Resist the devil, and he will flee from you. Draw near to God, and he will draw near to you. Cleanse your hands, you sinners, and purify your hearts, you double-minded.

James 4:7-8 ESV

Good Morning, Men of God!

It is impossible to stand against the enemy in our own strength. This "aged foe" has been fighting God's people since creation, and the only way we can hope to have victory is in full submission to God our Father in Heaven. The object of Satan's war against us can be anything. Whatever our personal area of weakness is will be the primary attack zone. With all the strength we have, all the ability and intelligence we possess, we do not have the ability to win the battle for our souls.

The standard (Isaiah 59:19) that the Lord promises to lift against the enemy begins with submitting to God, resisting the devil, and drawing near to God. That is our battle plan to stand against sin and temptation. Submission and resistance deals with the present battle. Drawing near to God through prayer, reading, serving, and worshipping cleanses us, preparing us for future battles. It aligns us with His provision of Godly power that enables us to stand in the time of attack.

Let us pray: *God, I cannot win the battle. Help me to always realize that. Only with You am I victorious. Father, I submit everything to You right now. I ask forgiveness for all of my sins and ask that You would cleanse my heart. I resist Satan, in the name of Jesus. He has to flee by Your power, God. Thank You, Father, for the freedom that comes in submitting to You. In Jesus Christ's name I pray, Amen.*

Love you guys,

Patrick

PRACTICING THANKSGIVING

Giving thanks always and for everything to God the Father in the name of our Lord Jesus Christ.

Ephesians 5:20 ESV

Good Morning, Men of God!

Regardless of what this week holds, we have so much to be thankful for. The lens that we view our lives through often dictates our attitude. Our attitude directly affects the attitudes of those we love. God has given husbands and fathers the ability to be the thermostat and not the thermometer in our homes.

Thankfulness is contagious, and it helps us to have the right perspective on life. Ephesians 5:20 calls us to be thankful always and for everything. Our joy is secure in Jesus Christ and the certain victory we have in this life because of Him. We have every reason to be thankful. Jesus lives! He loves you! Greater is He that is in you, than He that is in the world.

You have already overcome this week, through Jesus Christ. Give thanks!

Let us pray: *God, I am so thankful for You. Your love and compassion encompass me. Hallelujah, Lord! Help me to always have a spirit of thanksgiving that is contagious to all who are around me. I love You, Lord. Thank You for my life and daily provision. In Jesus Christ's name I pray, Amen.*

Love you guys,

Patrick

MERCY

For judgment is without mercy to one who has shown no mercy.
Mercy triumphs over judgment.

James 2:13 ESV

Good Morning, Men of God!

When is the last time you did something wrong, you made a mistake, a bad decision, or reacted in an ungodly way to a situation? When this happened, did God condemn you, or did you receive His mercy, provision, and forgiveness?

Christ died and was resurrected for the remission of your sins against God. As we deal with our wives and children this week, let's be sure to show them the same mercy in their time of error that God shows us. We put the mercy of God to us at risk when we don't show mercy to others. Our focus should be to imitate the kind of father God is to us, to our kids. Our focus should be to imitate the kind of husband He is to the Church, to our wives. Lovingly correct and rebuke when necessary, but remember the level of mercy we experience daily, and apply it to the loved ones around us.

Let us pray: *God, I could not live life without the mercy You so freely give. Guide me in being worthy of it by offering my family mercy in situations where they need it. Help me to lead with love, compassion, and understanding. Show me how to imitate Godly mercy on a daily basis to all those around me. Praise You, Lord. In Jesus Christ's name I pray, Amen.*

Love you guys,

Patrick

DAILY PURSUIT

O Lord, you have searched me and known me! Where shall I go from your Spirit? Or where shall I flee from your presence? If I ascend to heaven, you are there! If I make my bed in Sheol, you are there! If I take the wings of the morning and dwell in the uttermost parts of the sea, even there your hand shall lead me, and your right hand shall hold me.

Psalms 139:1, 7-10 ESV

Good Morning, Men of God!

We know that in Ephesians 5 we are commanded to love our wives as Christ loved the church. One of the most amazing things about our relationship with God is that He pursues us. We have nothing to offer Him, but He pursues us as if we are the most precious possession. He continually demonstrates His love to us.

Psalm 139 is just one example of scripture that shows how God is ever present and always pursuing us. As we look to replicate the relationship between Christ and the Church with the relationship between a husband and wife, we must ask ourselves if we are pursuing our wives. Are we taking time daily to make sure that she knows that we need, desire, and believe in her? We feel the love of God in an overwhelming fashion, daily. Our wives should feel pursued as God pursues us in Psalm 139. Think back to when you first met your spouse. Remember the way you felt, the passion you expressed, the desire you had to just be in her presence and hear her voice. Resurrect that desire and honor God in how you pursue your wife today.

Small tip: Most supermarkets have 3 for $12 flowers on sale. She won't care about the price, but getting flowers unexpectedly will make her feel pursued.

Let us pray: *Thank You, Father, for how you continually pursue me. Your love wraps me up completely and totally. Guide me in pursuing my wife and loving her in the way You love me. Help me to remember to pursue her daily. I want to make sure she feels the love that I have for her. Bless Your name, Jesus. In Jesus Christ's name I pray, Amen.*

Love you guys,

Patrick

LIFE ECHOING SALVATION

Therefore, we are ambassadors for Christ, God making his appeal through us. We implore you on behalf of Christ, be reconciled to God.

2 Corinthians 5:20 ESV

Good Morning, Men of God!

We send a message about what we believe in how we live and show love. Without saying a word, our actions and reactions to our environment demonstrate to others the strength of the source of our hope. We want to make sure that our words and our actions align. As a man of God, I can't say I live for Jesus, but also engage in vulgar conversation at work. I can't say I have salvation, but walk in a spirit of fear, depression, and worry. I can't say I am born again, but still participate willfully in sinful activities.

We are ambassadors for Christ. It is God's desire to use our lives to make an appeal to a lost world to be reconciled to Him. The world needs to look at us and see Jesus Christ. That view can be tainted if our actions don't match our words. Let's all ask God to examine us today. Are we being ambassadors for Christ in every part of our lives, or are there places we are still hanging on to that sin nature?

Let us pray: *God, our Father, thank You for calling me as Your ambassador. Please guide me in ensuring my life echoes what I believe and shows You as sovereign over my life. I do not want to be about words. Please allow my salvation to be communicated in how I live. Thank You, Lord. In Jesus Christ's name I pray, Amen.*

Love you guys,

Patrick

AFTERWORD

I remember the first time I ever met Pastor Patrick. He came to our church to ask some questions about our ministry, about pastoring in our particular area, and mostly just to ask us to pray for him and his church as he sought the Lord's will.

There were many things that struck me about Patrick that day.

He was exceptionally kind, respectful, and humble. He encouraged us with such genuine passion, pulling us to feel an instant kinship with him and shared purpose for our work in the world. There was an anointing on him; I could sense it even in that first interaction. The Spirit was with him, and his calling was deep and true.

The thing I remember most about that day was the way he spoke about his family. As he told us the story of their ministry, their moves, their losses and their victories, I was overcome with the sense of the depth of his love for his family, and especially his wife, Keisha. When he spoke of her, and of their partnership, his whole face lit up. I could see that his wife and children were the delight and joy of his life.

Soon, we invited Patrick and Keisha and Preservation Church to come be our roommates, to share our church building together. In some ways our communities were so different, and yet we knew that we needed each other. It was a holy, beautiful, life-changing partnership, where we learned from each other and encouraged each other and celebrated the beauty and diversity of our own unique callings, right on the same patch of earth.

Patrick changed me. He left me better than he found me. He challenged me to live every moment as an ambassador for Jesus.

Two weeks before Patrick went to be with Jesus, we had made an agreement for me to help him publish this book. He was so excited to begin the process of sharing these devotions with the men he was called to lead and to serve. I remember him telling me he had a hundred more books left in his heart to write, and I believed him. The Spirit spoke through Patrick, and his whole life was centered around sharing the love of Christ.

My heart is broken that we won't get to read a hundred more books written by Patrick. I am confident that they would have all been beautiful. But as I think of it, perhaps those hundred more books he had left were not manuscripts of words, but rather stories of the people who were impacted and influenced by his life. We who knew him have the books of our lives yet to be completed. How beautiful would it be for Patrick's leadership and legacy to continue to be a part of the stories of those still waiting to see him again in heaven?

As I have read Patrick's words in this book, I have been changed and challenged yet again. I hope that my story will continue on the path that Patrick travelled: a life devoted to the work of peace, restoration, healing, helping, compassion, and grace. A life devoted to Jesus.

I am so grateful for these words that have been preserved for a purpose.

May it be so.

Melody Farrell

For more information about

the life and legacy of Patrick Wesley Wheeler and his family,

please contact pwheelslegacy@gmail.com